HI!
HEY, JIMMY!
HEY,
JANUARY
1994

GOOD TO SEE YOU, MAN.
YOUR RESTAURANT LOOKS GREAT. LOVE THE NEW SIGN.

THANKS! HOW'S BUSINESS AT YOUR PLACE OUT IN GRANGEVIEW?

NEVER BETTER!
GOOD TO HEAR. RIGHT THIS WAY.
IT SMELLS SO GOOD!

A TOAST!
TO THE ROUNDVILLE ALL-STARS!
AND TO OUR CAPTAIN . . .
CAPTAIN
TO CHRISTINA!
CHRISTINA? YOU COMING?

YOU STILL WISH YOU MADE THE CHEER TEAM AT YOUR SCHOOL, HONEY?
ME? NAH.

I DON'T EVEN THINK ABOUT IT.

THIS IS GREAT! WE NEVER GO OUT TO EAT ALL THREE OF US!

IT'S SO NICE TO EAT AT SOMEONE ELSE'S RESTAURANT FOR A CHANGE.
SHIRLEY TEMPLE?
YES, PLEASE!

OOH, I LOVE THESE PLACEMATS!
CHINESE ZODIAC

HM, MAYBE WE SHOULD HAVE ZODIAC PLACEMATS AT GOLDEN DRAGON?
THEY'RE EXPENSIVE. I DON'T THINK THEY'RE IN OUR BUDGET.

I'M YEAR OF THE MONKEY. CURIOUS, BUT MISCHIEVOUS— YUP, SOUNDS LIKE ME!
WE NEED TO TALK ABOUT THE INSURANCE. I WROTE A CHECK, BUT THEY SAID THEY DIDN'T GET—

LET'S TALK LATER, OKAY? WHAT DO Y'ALL WANT? HUNAN BEEF?
OKAY, THIS IS HILARIOUS!

MOM, YOU'RE YEAR OF THE HORSE. AND DAD, YOU'RE A RAT.
THAT'S RIGHT—AMBITIOUS AND CHARMING.

IT SAYS "IF YOU'RE A RAT, NEVER MARRY A HORSE."
AND "IF YOU'RE A HORSE, MARRY **ANYONE** BUT A RAT."

HA-HA-HA! BOY, THESE THINGS SURE ARE WRONG SOMETIMES!

OOH, PEKING DUCK! MY FAVE!

THE SQ

UAD

WRITTEN BY **CHRISTINA SOONTORNVAT**

ILLUSTRATED BY **JOANNA CACAO**

COLORS BY WES DZIOBA

graphix

An Imprint of

SCHOLASTIC

SECOND SEMESTER OF EIGHTH GRADE

CHRISTINA! YOU READY?

READY!

THAT COAT DAD GOT YOU LOOKS NICE.
THANKS! I LOVE THIS FURRY COLLAR.

MAKES ME FEEL GLAMOROUS. LIKE GINGER ROGERS.
YOUR DAD ALWAYS HAD GOOD TASTE IN CLOTHES.

AH, TRAFFIC. BACK TO THE ROUTINE.
I'LL HAVE TO PRETEND I'M SAD WINTER BREAK IS OVER, BUT I'M SO GLAD TO BE GOING BACK.

REALLY?
YES! YOU AND DAD WORKED THE WHOLE TIME. I WAS DYING OF BOREDOM!

THINGS HAVE JUST BEEN HARDER THAN—
OOH, THERE'S MEGAN! BYE, MOM! LOVE YOU!

LEANNE! MEGAN!
YOU WORE THE NEW COAT! I LIKE IT.
IS THAT REAL FUR?
YUP, 100 PERCENT REAL SYNTHETIC FIBERS.

DID EITHER OF YOU GET A NEW SCHEDULE? THIS SEMESTER I HAVE HOME ECONOMICS.
IT'S EASY. THE HARDEST PART IS SEWING A PILLOW.

SEWING? I DON'T KNOW HOW TO SEW!
WHAT IF I GET A BAD GRADE? AND IT RUINS MY GPA?

GOOD ONE. NOW SHE'LL BE LIKE THIS ALL DAY.
I WON'T GET INTO NATIONAL HONOR SOCIETY, AND FORGET ABOUT ROTARY CLUB . . .

MEGAN: BEST FRIEND SINCE THIRD GRADE, IRANIAN AMERICAN, AWESOME GYMNAST.

LEANNE: NEW FRIEND SINCE LAST YEAR, STRAIGHT A++ STUDENT, SUMMER CAMP BIBLE VERSE CHAMP.

ME: PROUD THAI TEXAN, FANTASY AND SCI-FI FAN, LOVER OF OLD MOVIES, ON MY WAY TO HAVING THE BEST YEAR EVER.

WHAT'S WITH EVERYONE WEARING THOSE SAME SWEATSHIRTS?

THEIR YOUTH GROUP WENT ON A SKI TRIP OVER BREAK.
SOMEWHERE IN COLORADO.
WHAT DOES THAT SHIRT SAY?

CRESTED BUTTE
CRUSTED . . . BUTT?

IT'S CRESTED **BUTTE.** RHYMES WITH "CUTE." IT'S A TYPE OF MOUNTAIN.

OH YEAH, WE KNEW THAT.
YUP. LOVE THAT PLACE.
SO IMMATURE.

"CRUSTED BUTT"?
WHAT? THAT'S WHAT IT LOOKS LIKE!
I'M DYING!

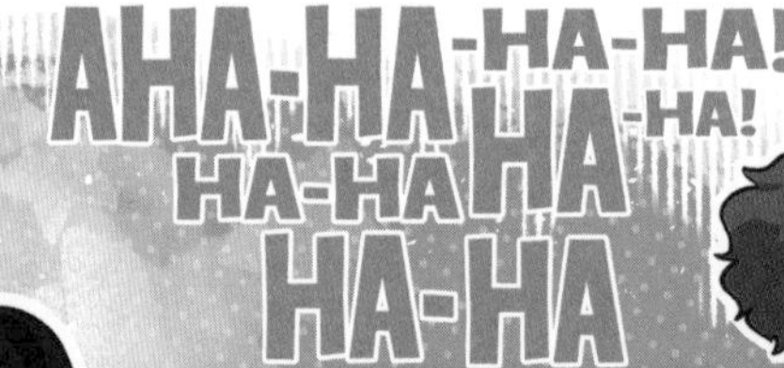
AHA-HA-HA-HA!
HA-HA HA-HA!
HA-HA

SEE YOU AT LUNCH!
HI, CHRISTINA! HOW WAS YOUR BREAK?
HEY, BRIN, IT WAS GOOD, THANKS. WHERE'S MS. HOBSON?
BROKE HER WRIST SKIING IN CRESTED BUTTE. WE'VE GOT A SUB ALL WEEK.
OH, GREAT.
I KNOW EXACTLY HOW THIS IS GOING TO GO.
SAY "HERE" WHEN I CALL YOUR NAME . . . DOROTHY MEANS . . . JEB POWERS . . .
HERE!
HERE!
CHRISTINA . . . SOO . . . SOO—

IT'S SOONTORNVAT.

WELL, NOW, THAT'S A LONG ONE. BUT DON'T WORRY, DEAR.

YOU COULD ALWAYS MARRY A BOY WITH A SHORTER LAST NAME.
HA-HA-H
HA-HA-H
HA-HA
YEAH, LIKE ROY ROACH!
HUH?

IF I MARRIED ROY ROACH . . .

HE COULD CHANGE **HIS** LAST NAME TO MINE.
WHAT?

OR WE COULD MASH THEM TOGETHER. LIKE ROACHTORNVAT. OR SOONTORNROACH.

"THE SOONTORNROACHES INVITE YOU TO A SOIREE AT THEIR MANSION."
HAS A NICE RING TO IT, RIGHT?
HA-HA! I LOVE IT!
I LITERALLY HAVE NO IDEA WHAT'S GOING ON RIGHT NOW.

ALL RIGHT, SETTLE DOWN!
HA-HA HA
HA-HA HA-HA

I CAN TELL YOU'RE A UNIQUE ONE, DEAR.

IT'S TRUE, I WAS UNIQUE.

FOR ONE THING, I WAS ONE OF THE ONLY ASIAN AMERICAN KIDS IN OUR SMALL TEXAS TOWN.

ART ROOM
IN SEVENTH GRADE, I NEVER WANTED TO STAND OUT.

BUT THIS YEAR, I WAS STARTING TO FEEL MORE CONFIDENT BEING MYSELF.
WELCOME BACK, ART COMRADES.
I THINK YOU MEAN ADVANCED ART COMRADES, CARRIE.

LESLIE, HOW WAS YOUR SOLSTICE?
I'VE NEVER BEEN SO HAPPY TO SEE PEOPLE WHO ARE NOT MY FAMILY.
SAME. MY SISTER'S BOYFRIEND CAME OVER EVERY DAY. SO ANNOYING.

MINE WAS BORING. I JUST WATCHED MOVIES AND ATE THAI FOOD.
YEAH, SO ROUGH.
BRAGGER!
ALL RIGHT, EVERYONE, LET'S GET STARTED.
THIS SEMESTER YOU'LL WORK WITH YOUR TABLE GROUP TO COLLABORATE ON A POTTERY PROJECT.
EACH INDIVIDUAL PIECE SHOULD STAND ON ITS OWN . . .
BUT TOGETHER, THE IMPACT SHOULD BE EVEN STRONGER.
SO, WHAT SHOULD WE DO?
WHAT IF WE SCULPT TOY ARMY MEN, BUT THEY'RE ALL MELTING?
HM, LIKE AN ANTI-WAR THING?
TOO OBVIOUS. WE NEED TO REALLY PUSH THE ENVELOPE HERE.

WHAT ABOUT . . .

TOES.
EW! TOES?

A THOUSAND CERAMIC TOES.
LIKE A TOE FOREST?

TOES ARE SO DISTURBING.
IT'S WEIRD. I ABSOLUTELY LOVE IT.
BUT WHAT ARE WE TRYING TO SAY?

TOE-GETHER, ANYTHING IS POSSIBLE.
THERE IS NO I IN TOE.

"TOE BE, OR NOT TOE BE. THAT IS THE QUESTION."
YES!
SOMEONE'S CREATIVE JUICES ARE FLOWING THIS MORNING!

I'M SO EXCITED ABOUT OUR PROJECT!
NOW EVERYWHERE I LOOK, ALL I SEE ARE TOES.
TOMORROW, LET'S START SCULPTING!

ROOM 128
Homew
P17
Q2-14
P19
Q5-24
SEE YOU LATER!
BYE! LATER!
SO FAR, EIGHTH GRADE WAS AWESOME.

GOOD CLASSES.
Homew
P17
Q2-14
P19
Q5-24

GREAT FRIENDS.

TEACHERS, PLEASE TAKE YOUR CLASSES TO THE GYM FOR OUR WELCOME BACK PEP RALLY!

I HAD EVERYTHING I WANTED.

EXCEPT FOR ONE THING.
ALL RIGHT, BULLS, LET'S GIVE IT UP . . .

FOR YOUR EIGHTH GRADE CHEERLEADING SQUAD!

COME ON 'HORNS!
SHOW US SOME SPIRIT!
SIGH . . .
ONE AND TWO AND THREE AND FOUR . . .

BOOM-BOOM-BOOM!

SHAKE THE ROOM, SHAKE THE ROOM!

SHAKE IT UP AND LET IT GO . . .

BOOM!

BOOM-BOOM-
BOOM-BOOM!
SHAKE
THE ROOM!
BOOM!
FRIDAY NIGHT

NOT BAD FOR MEMORIZING THOSE MOVES JUST THE OTHER DAY.
ARE WE LOSERS?

BECAUSE WE LEARN ALL THE CHEER DANCES EVEN THOUGH WE DIDN'T MAKE THE SQUAD? NAH.
DON'T YOU WISH YOU COULD TIME TRAVEL TO LAST YEAR AND TRY AGAIN?

UGH, AND RELIVE TRYING OUT IN FRONT OF OUR **WHOLE** GRADE?

I WISH IT ALL THE TIME. IF WE HAD MADE IT . . .

THE OTHER KIDS WOULD RESPECT US.
THE CUTE BOYS WOULD SIT AT OUR LUNCH TABLE.
WE'D BE PART OF A REAL SQUAD.

WELL, TRYOUTS FOR THE NINTH GRADE SQUAD ARE IN APRIL . . .
FORGET ABOUT IT.
ALL THE CURRENT CHEERLEADERS WILL MAKE IT. AND THERE AREN'T ANY EXTRA SPOTS.
OH.
WE'LL JUST HAVE TO FIND SOMETHING ELSE TO BE OUR THING.
WHAT, LIKE "ART"?
WHAT'S THAT SUPPOSED TO MEAN?
NOTHING. JUST THAT YOUR ART FRIENDS THINK THEY'RE TOO COOL FOR EVERYONE ELSE.

THAT'S NOT TRUE! AND WHAT ABOUT YOU? ARE YOU GOING TO DITCH US NEXT YEAR FOR YOUR GYMNASTICS FRIENDS?
NO . . .
HEY, ISN'T ANYONE WORRIED ABOUT ME DITCHING THEM FOR THE ACADEMIC NERDS?
YOU **ARE** THE ACADEMIC NERD.
YEAH, PARTY OF ONE.
LEANNE, YOU'RE TOO WOUND UP. HERE, HAVE A STRESS BALL.
THANKS.
NOOOOOOOO!

GAH! ACK . . . !
WHAT'S THAT
SMELL?
I SHOULD HAVE
WARNED YOU. **NEVER**
SQUEEZE MEGAN'S
STRESS BALL.

IT'S LIKE BEING
INSIDE THE BOWELS OF
AN ELEPHANT.
YUP, THAT'S
MY SPECIAL FART-
CAPTURE BALL.

FIRST I
SQUEEZE THE
BALL . . .

THEN I
RELEASE THE BALL AT THE
SAME MOMENT I RELEASE
MY GAS.

THE ODOR SOAKS INTO THE FOAM, LOCKED IN UNTIL YOU SQUEEZE AGAIN.
THAT IS DEMENTED.

LET ME TRY IT!
REMEMBER TO RELEASE SLOWLY . . .
HOLD ON!

Y'ALL. WE ARE **EIGHTH** GRADERS. DON'T YOU THINK IT'S ABOUT TIME WE GROW UP A LITTLE?

GIMME THAT BALL.
YOU HOLD HER DOWN, I'LL DO THE SQUISHING.

GAH! AHA-HA! LET GO OF ME!
YOU WANT MATURE? I GOT SOME MATURE GAS READY TO GO.

CHRISTINA! ARE YOU UP?
COMING!
FEBRUARY
OH, THAT'S SWEET— DAD GOT YOU A ROSE FOR VALENTINE'S.
OH, UH, ACTUALLY THAT'S FOR YOU. FROM ME. HAPPY VALENTINE'S, SWEETIE.
AW THANKS, MOM! WHERE IS DAD, BY THE WAY?
OH GOSH, I'VE GOT TO GET TO THE RESTAURANT FOR A DELIVERY. WE NEED TO GO!
READY!

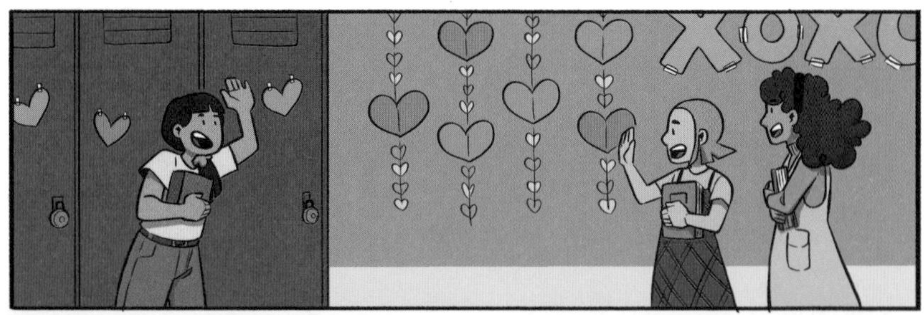

XOXO
LOVE
Nice
Sweet
U R CUTE
Be KIND
BFF
CUTE
XOXO
HUG me
LOVE

SUPPORT YOUR STUDENT COUNCIL!

SEND A FLOWER TO YOUR CRUSH!

$1 CARNATION Fundraiser

DARN, I ONLY HAVE TWENTY-FIVE CENTS.
WHO DO YOU WANT TO SEND ONE TO?

I KNOW . . .
SHHH!
WHO?!

COLT RAINEY!
OOOOOH, COLT? REALLY?
WHEN HE ASKS TO BORROW MY CALCULATOR IT FEELS LIKE MY GUTS ARE FLOATING INSIDE MY BODY.
MAYBE COLT SHOULD KNOW THAT HE HAS A SECRET ADMIRER.
YEAH, WE COULD SEND HIM A CARNATION SIGNED, "YOU MAKE MY GUTS FLOAT. LOVE, LEANNE."
I WILL DESTROY YOU AND THEY WILL NEVER FIND THE BODY.
HA-HA, OKAY, OKAY, WE WERE KIDDING!
RELAX!

I'M DOING IT! I'M SENDING ONE TO ANDY DERMOND!
OH MY GOSH!
$1
CARN

BUT HE'S GOING OUT WITH STACY!
I DON'T CARE. I JUST WANT HIM TO FEEL LOVED.

UGH. ANDY DERMOND? WHY IS EVERYONE OBSESSED WITH HIM?
ANDY GOT CUTE IN FOURTH GRADE AND HAS INCREASED IN CUTE FACTOR EVERY YEAR.

THOSE GIRLS ARE DREAMING. ANDY IS PRACTICALLY ENGAGED TO STACY.

HERE HE COMES!

GREAT HAIR. REALLY NICE TEETH.

AND DESTINED TO MARRY THE MOST POPULAR GIRL IN SCHOOL.

STACY KISER:
PERFECT CLOTHES. PERFECT SMILE. PERFECT LIFE.

OH, ANDY! THEY'RE BEAUTIFUL!

OH, GAG.

COLOR
THEORY
. . . AND THEN HE WHIPS OUT THIS HUGE BOUQUET OF LILIES!
LILIES ARE A SYMBOL OF DEATH.

YOU'RE TALKING ABOUT ANDY'S BOUQUET, TOO?
I WAS IN PRE-K WITH ANDY. HE USED TO EAT PASTE LIKE IT WAS COOL WHIP.

CARNATION DELIVERY!
COLOR
THEORY

THEN THERE'S THE CARNATION: SYMBOL OF DESPERATION.
NOTHING SAYS TRUE LOVE LIKE A WILTED FLOWER.
YEAH, WHO WOULD WANT THAT?

FOR ME?

FOR US? HUH?

"WHEN I'M WITH YOU, I CAN'T SEE THE FOREST FOR THE TOES."
"I'M TOE-TALLY INTO YOU."

"X'S AND TOES"?
GREG!
NICE ONE!
WHAT CAN I SAY? I'M A HOPELESS TOE-MANTIC.

THAT FRIDAY NIGHT
LET'S GO LADY BULLS!

MORE KIDS HAD STARTED "GOING OUT" THIS YEAR.

SUDDENLY, SO MANY GIRLS HAD BOYFRIENDS.

THE MAIN BOY IN MY LIFE WAS GREG.

ARE YOU SCARED OF A BUTTERFLY?
NO . . .
I LOVED GREG, BUT I DIDN'T **LIKE**-LIKE HIM.

CLAP!
THEN WHY'D YOU BLINK?
UGH, THAT JOKE IS FROM LIKE SECOND GRADE.

ARE YOU SCARED OF A GLACIER?
NO . . .

YOU BLINKED! YOU'RE SCARED OF A GLACIER!
YOU ARE SO ANNOYING.
HA-HA-HA-HA-HA!

ARE YOU SCARED OF A SLOTH?
WILL YOU KNOCK IT OFF?

MVP
LET'S GET SEATS UP HIGH!

SOME OF THE OTHER BOYS AT SCHOOL COULD BE SO MEAN.

LAST YEAR, TOBIN WAS RELENTLESS.

WHY DON'T YOU GO BACK TO CHINA?

CHING CHONG, BING BONG, RICE GIRL!

HEY, CHRISTINA!

WHAT?
YOU DROPPED YOUR TICKET.

ANNND?
NOTHING. THAT'S IT.

WHAT'S HER PROBLEM?
YEAH, RICE GIRL, CHILL OUT!

WHAT WAS ALL THAT ABOUT?
NOTHING, I JUST HATE THOSE GUYS.

ME TOO.
REALLY?

OF COURSE. BUT THEY'RE NOT EVEN WORTH ONE OF OUR LITTLE TOES.
YOU'RE SO RIGHT!
CHRISTINA!

MEGAN! I DIDN'T THINK YOU COULD COME!
MY PARENTS CHANGED THEIR MINDS.

CHRISTINA, UP HERE! WE FOUND AN EMPTY ROW!
COME SIT WITH US!

NAH, YOU'RE WITH YOUR ART FRIENDS.
DON'T BE SILLY. COME ON!

ISN'T THIS GREAT? ALL OF US TOGETHER!
UH, HI.
UH, HI.
BE AGGRESSIVE! B-E AGGRESSIVE!
B-E A-G-G!
R-E-S-S!
I-V-E!

OH, LOOK, THE CHEERLEADERS CAN SPELL!

IT'S LIKE SESAME STREET, BUT WITH POM-POMS!
HA-HA!

WHY DO THEY EVEN COME TO THE GAME IF THEY HATE EVERYTHING ABOUT IT?
THEY'RE JUST KIDDING.
AND THAT'S THE END OF THE FIRST QUARTER!

I'M GOING TO DIE WITHOUT FRITO PIE! CHRISTINA, ARE YOU COMING?
UH, I'LL STAY HERE. BRING ME A COKE?

SO, DO YOU THINK THEY'LL DO ANY STUNTS AT HALFTIME?
OH, SO **NOW** WE CAN TALK ABOUT CHEERLEADING?

OH, STOP IT . . . HEY, HOW COME THERE'S ONLY SEVEN GIRLS? WHERE'S STEPHANIE?

SHE'S ON THE COURT—DUH!

OH RIGHT! I FORGOT SHE PLAYS BASKETBALL!

OH MY GOSH, SHE'S SO GOOD.

NOT JUST GOOD. THE BEST ONE ON THE TEAM.
24
16
08

THE RUMOR IS SHE'S GOING TO MAKE THE HIGH SCHOOL VARSITY TEAM AS A NINTH GRADER.
WOW, I HAD NO IDEA.

IF SHE DOES, SHE'LL BE TOO BUSY TO CHEER.
OH.

BEVERLY IS MOVING, AND MANDY ISN'T TRYING OUT BECAUSE SHE DOESN'T GET ALONG WITH THE GIRLS.
SO THAT MEANS . . .

THREE SPOTS. THREE OF US. YOU, ME, AND LEANNE.
BUT TRYING OUT **AGAIN?** DON'T YOU REMEMBER HOW SCARY THAT WAS?

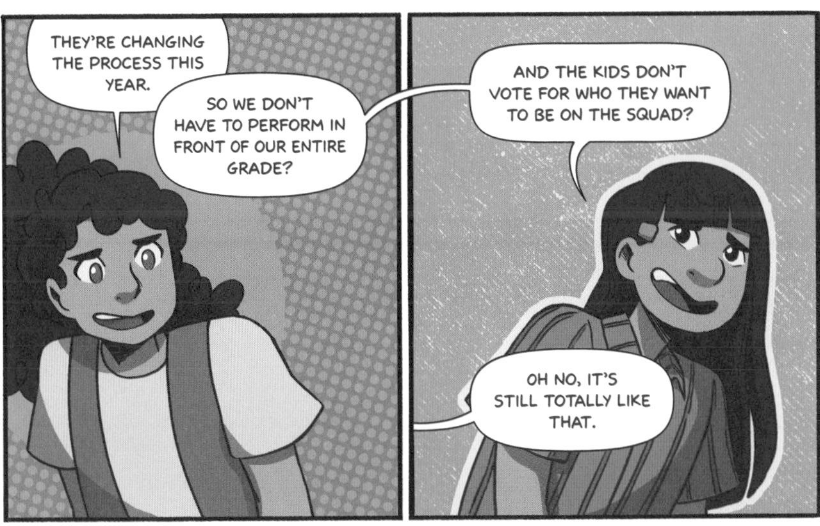
THEY'RE CHANGING THE PROCESS THIS YEAR.
SO WE DON'T HAVE TO PERFORM IN FRONT OF OUR ENTIRE GRADE?
AND THE KIDS DON'T VOTE FOR WHO THEY WANT TO BE ON THE SQUAD?
OH NO, IT'S STILL TOTALLY LIKE THAT.

BUT NOW THE JUDGES' SCORES AND STUDENTS' VOTES COUNT EQUALLY. SO IT'S NOT JUST A POPULARITY CONTEST.
DO YOU THINK WE HAVE A CHANCE?

WE'VE BEEN PRACTICING THE CHEERS ALL YEAR. I KNOW WE DO!
SHH, LET'S TALK LATER.

WE'RE BACK! I GOT YOU A SPIRIT HAT. TO BE WORN WITH SARCASM, OBVIOUSLY.
FRITO PIE IS THE BEST THING HUMANS EVER INVENTED.

BITE?
UH, SURE!
NO THANKS.

BUT STEPHANIE'S THE SQUAD CAPTAIN. SHE WOULDN'T GIVE THAT UP, RIGHT?
YOU HAVE ALGEBRA WITH HER. ASK HER YOURSELF.

BUT DON'T SKIP OUT ON THIS CHANCE JUST BECAUSE YOU WANT TO ACT COOL.
I'M NOT! I'LL ASK HER MONDAY.

BYE! AND DON'T FORGET— MONDAY!
I WON'T!
VOLUNTEER

Y'ALL WAITING FOR YOUR RIDE?
YES, MA'AM. MY MOM DRIVES A RED CAR.
VOLUNTEER

I SEE HER, SWEETIE. OVER THERE.
REALLY? WHERE?

RIGHT THERE.

OH, THAT'S . . . NOT MY MOM.
VOLUNTEER

CHRISTINA!

THAT'S HER. THANKS, THOUGH.
OLUNTEER

HOW WAS THE GAME?
I THINK WE MAY HAVE WON? OR LOST. ONE OF THE TWO.
THE FRITO PIE WAS OUTSTANDING.

IT WASN'T THE FIRST TIME SOMEONE HAD GOTTEN THINGS MIXED UP WITH ME AND MY MOM.

CHECK THIS OUT!
COOL!
HEY, ARE YOU ADOPTED?
NO.
ARE YOU SURE? YOU DON'T LOOK LIKE YOUR MOM.
HOLD ON.
AM I ADOPTED?

ARE YOU MY REAL MOM?
SWEETIE, DON'T BE SILLY—OF COURSE I AM!

ARE YOU **SURE** YOU'RE MY REAL MOM?
CHRISTINA, WHY ARE YOU ASKING ME THIS?

JAKE ASKED IF I WAS ADOPTED. BECAUSE WE DON'T LOOK ALIKE.
FIRST OF ALL, EVEN IF YOU WERE ADOPTED I WOULD **STILL** BE YOUR REAL MOM.

BUT YOU'RE NOT ADOPTED. HERE. THIS WAS TAKEN WHEN WE BROUGHT YOU HOME FROM THE HOSPITAL.

YOU WERE ADORABLE.
EW, I LOOK LIKE A FROG!

THE OLDER I GOT, THE MORE I SAW WHAT MOM AND I HAD IN COMMON.
DIMPLES, ROUND CHEEKS, BIG SMILE

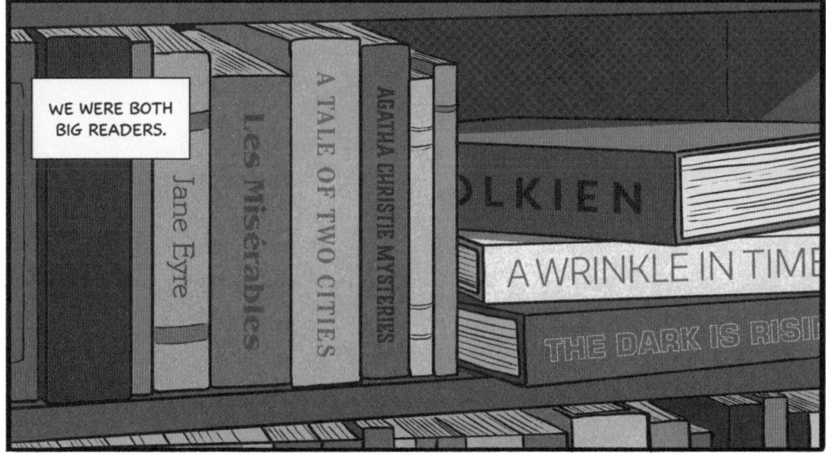

WE WERE BOTH BIG READERS.
Jane Eyre
Les Misérables
A TALE OF TWO CITIES
AGATHA CHRISTIE MYSTERIES
LKIEN
A WRINKLE IN TIM
THE DARK IS RISI

AND WE BOTH LOVED OLD MOVIES.
POPCORN'S READY!

IT'S ALMOST STARTING! MOM, WHAT ARE YOU LOOKING AT?
JUST WONDERING WHERE YOUR DAD IS. HE SHOULD BE HOME.

COME ON.
WE CAN'T MISS
OUR SUNDAY
NIGHT RITUAL.

WHO'S
YOUR FAVORITE
OLD HOLLYWOOD
COUPLE?
WELL, THERE'S
FRED AND GINGER . . .

AND SPENCER
AND KATE ARE GREAT,
OF COURSE.

MY FAVORITE ACTOR
IS GENE KELLY, HANDS
DOWN. HE CAN SING, ACT,
DANCE . . .

HE IS
EVERYTHING!

GENE AND CHRISTINA STAR IN
DANCING THROUGH INCLEMENT WEATHER
MUSIC!
PASSION!
TAP-DANCING!
DANCE WITH ME!
BUT IT'S RAINING!
DON'T WORRY. MY HAIR WILL REMAIN PERFECT.
AHHHHHH . . .
MOM, THAT HAD THE PERFECT HAPPY ENDING! WHY ARE YOU CRYING?
SORRY, THIS ONE JUST GETS TO ME, I GUESS.

MONDAY AFTERNOON
ALGEBRA HOMEWORK DUE WEDNESDAY!
NOW'S MY CHANCE.
HEY, CHRISTINA. DID YOU FINISH THE HOMEWORK?
UM, NOT YET.
SO, STEPHANIE . . . I HEARD THAT MAYBE, WELL . . .
IS THIS ABOUT THE SQUAD? NOPE, I'M NOT TRYING OUT AGAIN. I ALREADY TOLD COACH MONROE.
WHY NOT?
I WANT TO PLAY BASKETBALL NEXT YEAR, AND IT'LL BE TOO HARD TO DO BOTH.
AND THERE'S ANOTHER REASON. DON'T TELL ANYONE . . .

CHEERLEADING'S OKAY, BUT I DON'T LOVE IT.
YOU DON'T?

WHEN I'M CHEERING, I FEEL LIKE I'M PLAYING A PART. LIKE I'M NOT MY REAL SELF. MAKE SENSE?

YEAH, IT DOES. AND IT'S VERY MATURE OF YOU TO REALIZE THAT.

AND IT MEANS THERE'S ONE MORE OPEN SPOT!

BRRRING
BAKE SALE

Y'ALL!

IT'S TRUE. SHE'S NOT TRYING OUT AGAIN.
WELL?
OH MY GOSH! IT'S A SIGN!

WE MIGHT NEVER GET ANOTHER CHANCE.
YES, LET'S DO IT!
I'M IN!
TRYOUT SIGN UP

FRIDAY
I WAS **DEFINITELY** MAKING THE SQUAD THIS TIME.
GOLDEN DRAGON
CHINESE RESTAURANT
LET'S HEAR IT!

THAT MEANT PRACTICING EVERY DAY.
THE RED AND . . .
THE WHITE!

CHRISTINA? WE'RE ABOUT TO OPEN AND I NEED THE NAPKINS!
UH, OKAY, MOM!

HEY, UNCLE WALTER. HI, SAM!
HEY THERE!
HI, CHRISTINA!
PLEASE WAIT TO BE SEATED

THE BEST PERK OF MY FAMILY OWNING A RESTAURANT.

OKAY, ACTUALLY **THIS** IS THE BEST PERK.

DON'T WORRY, I WON'T TELL YOUR UNCLE WALTER.
ACK!

HA-HA, THANKS, ANTONIO!
HOW'S SCHOOL?

GREAT! I THINK THIS YEAR IS GOING TO BE THE BEST—
WE'VE TALKED ABOUT THIS BEFORE!

YOU CAN'T JUST GIVE AWAY THE SHRIMP. THEY'RE FORTY DOLLARS A BOX.
IT'S JUST ONE BOX. AND I KNOW HOW MUCH IT COSTS.
YOU NEVER—
YOU ALWAYS—
BRRRRRING!!!
CHRISTINA! PHONE CALL FOR YOU.
OH, THANKS, I'LL TAKE IT!
OH, HEY, MEGAN! TOMORROW? A SLEEPOVER?

SURE, MY MOM CAN BRING ME! NO, SHE'S NOT BUSY . . .
I **AM** BUSY, ACTUALLY. I'M WORKING HERE.
SO MY DAD CAN BRING ME . . .
YOU CAN'T SLEEP OVER TOMORROW, HONEY.
WE HAVE THE THAI ASSOCIATION DINNER IN DALLAS.
TOMORROW?! BUT IT'S OUR BUSIEST NIGHT.
WE HAVE TO GO. I'M THE PRESIDENT THIS YEAR.
SORRY, I CAN'T . . . YEAH, GOTTA DO A THAI THING . . . OKAY, BYE.

SATURDAY NIGHT
WE CAN'T STAY LATE. WE HAVE TO GET TO THE RESTAURANT EARLY . . .
I CAN'T JUST LEAVE IN THE MIDDLE OF THINGS . . .

YOU NEVER . . .
YOU ALWAYS . . .

SAWASDEE KRUB, MISTER PRESIDENT!
WADDEE KRUB!
CHRISTINA! YOU GOT SO BIG!
SAWASDEE KA, AUNTIE.
SAWASDEE KA! LONG TIME NO SEE!
SAWASDEE KA! IT'S BEEN TOO LONG!
CHRISTINA!

THANK YOU, THANK YOU, EVERYONE! I'M HONORED TO BE YOUR PRESIDENT!
GO, SHORTY!
YOU'RE THE MAN!
SPEECH, SPEECH!

เย็นนี้เรา เข้ามาร่วมกันเป็น ครอบครัว...

YOUR DAD IS SUCH A GOOD SPEAKER.
REALLY? I DON'T SPEAK THAI, SO I DON'T REALLY KNOW WHAT HE'S SAYING.

BUT YOU CAN TELL HE'S GOOD WITH THE CROWD, RIGHT?
YEAH, I GUESS I CAN.

IF HE STAYED BACK IN THAILAND, HE'D BE A BIG SHOT BY NOW.
A BIG SHOT?

RICH. MAKING CONNECTIONS. IT'S A SHAME, REALLY.
WELL, OUR RESTAURANT **WAS** VOTED BEST ASIAN FOOD IN GRANGEVIEW THIS YEAR . . .
ALL RIGHT, ENOUGH WITH THE TALKING . . .
IT'S TIME TO JAM!

SHH! QUICK, UNDER HERE!
AW, THIS IS JUST LIKE WHEN WE WERE LITTLE!

"TAKE ME HOME . . . COUNTRY ROAD . . ."
AT LEAST THE MUSIC IS A LITTLE MUFFLED UNDER HERE.
AND THE BEST PART IS—

EASY ACCESS!
OOH, RAMBUTAN! GET ME ONE!
AND GRAB SOME LONGANS!

THAI FRUITS ARE THE BEST, RIGHT?
WE DON'T HAVE ASIAN MARKETS IN GRANGEVIEW.

HOW DO YOU SURVIVE?
IT'S A DAILY TEST OF COURAGE.

AND THAI DESSERTS!
WE SHOULD START A THAI KIDS CLUB. AND EAT FRUIT AT EVERY MEETING.
YES! AND WE CAN COLLECT CUTE STICKERS AND ERASERS!

I'M NOT JOINING IF WE HAVE TO EAT STINKY DURIAN.
HA-HA, I LOVE DURIAN!

CHRISTINA, YOU CAN ONLY COME TO HALF THE MEETINGS.
WHAT? WHY?

BECAUSE YOU'RE ONLY A LUUK KHRUENG.
YEAH, YOU'RE JUST A HALF KID!

HA-HA, VERY FUNNY.
OH SHUT UP, THAT'S NOT COOL.

BYE! SAWASDEE JA! JER GAN, KAP!
DON'T BE A STRANGER!
JER GAN!
BYE!
AM I JUST A "HALF KID"?
BUT WHICH HALF AM I?
"IN GRANGEVIEW, I STAND OUT FOR BEING ASIAN . . ."
GO BACK TO CHINA!
"WITH OUR THAI FRIENDS, I'M NOT ASIAN ENOUGH."
YOU CAN ONLY COME TO HALF THE MEETINGS!

WELL, I'M NOT LETTING THEM GET TO ME.

OUR FAMILY IS PERFECT, JUST THE WAY WE ARE.

I LOVE YOU!

THE NEXT SATURDAY

OKAY, THAT TIME WE WERE FLAWLESS!
I COULD DO THAT IN MY SLEEP.

I'VE BEEN PRACTICING MY JUMPS. WANT TO SEE?

YES!

WHOA, YOU HAVE GOTTEN SO MUCH BETTER!
HOW DO YOU DO THAT?

I IMAGINE THAT MY FEET ARE FULL OF HELIUM AND THEY JUST WANT TO FLY UP!
BE RIGHT BACK. GRABBING DRINKS!
I ♥ TX

THANKS FOR BEING MY PARTNER THIS YEAR. ARE YOU SAD THAT MEGAN'S TRYING OUT WITH ALLIE AGAIN?
IT'S FINE.

ALLIE AND MEGAN CAN BOTH TUMBLE, SO THEY MAKE A GOOD PAIR.

I CAN'T TUMBLE. AND MY JUMPS ARE NOWHERE NEAR AS GOOD AS YOURS.
BUT YOUR VOICE IS SO STRONG.
I ♥ TX

YES! IT IS! RIGHT!

SEE? BE THAT LOUD AND DON'T MESS UP, AND YOU'LL MAKE IT.
YOU THINK SO?

YES! NO ONE PRACTICES MORE THAN US.
THAT'S FOR SURE. DID Y'ALL HEAR WHAT THE POPULAR KIDS ARE DOING TONIGHT?
NO, WHAT?

GOING TO A PARTY AT CLAY HENCKELL'S HOUSE. RUMOR IS THERE'S GOING TO BE "PHYSICAL ACTIVITY."

LIKE ROLLER BLADING?
TABLE TENNIS?
I ♥ TX

NO! I MEAN KISSING!
OH, RIGHT.
I KNEW THAT.
I ♥ TX

I'M NOT KISSING OR DATING ANYONE UNTIL AFTER COLLEGE.
YEAH RIGHT! IF COLT RAINEY WANTED TO DATE YOU, YOU'D SAY NO?

I'D DATE SOMEONE IF THEY ASKED ME OUT.
OKAY, MAYBE ONLY COLT . . .
I ♥ TX

YOU **WOULD???**
WHO? **WHO?**

I DON'T KNOW! GENE KELLY?
THAT NEW KID IN OUR SCIENCE CLASS?

DO YOU WANT TO SEE HIM?
YES!

TAKE YOUR PICK. WE'VE GOT AN AMERICAN IN PARIS OR BRIGADOON!
OH, COME ON!
REMIND ME TO BRING THE MOVIES FROM NOW ON.
I ♥ TX

CAN YOU BELIEVE WE'RE TRYING OUT AGAIN?
KIND OF?
YES.
WE HAVE TO PROMISE EACH OTHER THAT IF WE MAKE IT, WE WON'T START ACTING DIFFERENT.
YOU MEAN LIKE WE'RE BETTER THAN EVERYONE ELSE?
HEY, THINGS WILL BE DIFFERENT, BUT IN A GOOD WAY.
IF WE MAKE IT, LIFE WILL GO FROM GOOD TO . . .
"PERFECT."
SHE HAD EVERYTHING SHE EVER WANTED!

BYE! CALL ME TOMORROW!
I WILL!
MOM, I'M HOME!
MY LEGS ARE SO SORE! WE PRACTICED OUR JUMPS FOR HOURS!
NOT TO BRAG, BUT I THINK I HAVE A GOOD SHOT THIS YEAR. I'M FEELING LIKE . . .
MOM?

SO WHO'S GOING TO TELL HER?
WE SHOULD TELL HER TOGETHER.
I DON'T WANT TO MAKE HER UPSET. IT COULD MESS UP HER GRADES.
WE CAN'T LIE TO HER. SHE HAS TO KNOW THE TRUTH.
ARE WE REALLY SURE?
I CAN'T KEEP DOING THIS ANYMORE. I KNOW WE BOTH AGREE—
THIS MARRIAGE WAS OVER A LONG TIME AGO.

OVER???
DO YOU EVEN KNOW WHAT YOU'RE SAYING?
WE WERE PLANNING TO TELL YOU . . .
YOU CANNOT DO THIS!

HONEY—
LEAVE ME ALONE!
WHAT IS HAPPENING?

NOTHING MADE SENSE.

MOM TRIED TO EXPLAIN.
WHEN WE FIRST MET . . .
BUT NOW . . . LITIGATION
BORROWING MONEY
UNRELIABLE
IRRECONCILABLE DIFFERENCES

I STILL DIDN'T GET IT.
NEVER HOME
RISKY INVESTMENTS
LOVE DOESN'T ALWAYS
LAWYERS OVERSPENDING
YEARS AGO
ONE TIME I FOUND OUT . . .

STOP TALKING!
JUST STOP!

I **DON'T** WANT THIS.
I DON'T, EITHER, BUT SOMETIMES PEOPLE GET D—
NO!
IT IS NOT HAPPENING!
IT'S JUST **NOT** HAPPENING.

WHERE ARE YOU GOING?
OH, UM, WELL, HONEY . . .

I'M GOING TO STAY AT SAM'S WHILE WE FIGURE THINGS OUT.

WHAT DOES THAT MEAN?
I . . . DON'T KNOW . . .

CHRISTINA . . .
YEAH?

I'M SORRY, HONEY . . .

FINE. I DON'T WANT TO TALK TO YOU, EITHER.

THE NEXT DAY AFTER SCHOOL.
THINGS IMMEDIATELY GOT WEIRD.

AREN'T YOU COMING IN?
NO, I HAVE TO . . . UM, GO TO THE BANK.
YOUR DAD'S INSIDE, THOUGH. HE'LL GIVE YOU A RIDE HOME.
MY DAD? WHY NOT JUST CALL HIM DAD?

SAWASDEE KA!
WADDEE KRUB!

HEY, SAM? IS MY DAD HERE?

UM, YEAH . . . I THINK SO.
ISN'T HE STAYING WITH YOU?

UH, YEAH, YEAH, HE IS! YOU WANT SOMETHING TO EAT?
NO THANKS, I'M NOT HUNGRY.

HERE, HAVE A FORTUNE COOKIE.
AREN'T THESE ONLY FOR CUSTOMERS?

HAVE A COKE! EXTRA CHERRIES!
OKAY, WHAT IS UP WITH EVERYONE?

DAD!
OH, HEY, HONEY!

HOW LONG ARE YOU STAYING AT SAM'S?
OH, SAM'S? YEAH, WELL . . .
YOU'D LIKE HIS APARTMENT, HONEY. HE'S GOT A BIG POOL, AND—
BUT WHEN ARE YOU COMING BACK HOME?

EVENING, FOLKS! TABLE FOR FOUR?
OH, WE'RE OPEN! I BETTER GO HELP OUT.

WELCOME, FOLKS! THE USUAL TABLE?
PSST HEY, WE GOT A PROBLEM!

WHAT IS IT?
THE DISHWASHER BROKE DOWN!
THAT'S THE THIRD TIME THIS MONTH.

DINA, CAN YOU HELP IN THE BACK AND WASH THEM BY HAND?
I CAN!
ORDER UP!

WHERE'S THAT BARBECUE CHICKEN?
YOU DIDN'T PUNCH THE TICKET!
IT'S GETTING BUSY OUT THERE . . .
UGH, OKAY—FIRE IT RIGHT AWAY. I'LL GO STALL THEM!
SHRIMP LO-MEIN COMING UP!

SOME PEOPLE SAY THAT A GOOD RESTAURANT IS LIKE A SWAN . . .
MORE ICED TEA?
EVENING, FOLKS. GOT YOUR FAVORITE TABLE RIGHT HERE.

GLIDING ELEGANTLY OVER THE SURFACE OF A LAKE . . .
YOUR ORDER IS ON THE WAY. HAVE SOME EGG ROLLS WHILE YOU WAIT, ON THE HOUSE.

BUT UNDERNEATH THE WATER, ITS FEET ARE PADDLING LIKE CRAZY.
ORDER UP!
I NEED THAT BARBECUE CHICKEN NOW!
THE REPAIRMAN CAN'T BE HERE UNTIL TOMORROW!

I THINK OF IT MORE LIKE A MOVIE SET. YOU PUT ON A SHOW FOR YOUR CUSTOMERS.

YOU WANT THEM TO BE HAPPY.

AND YOU NEVER LET THEM KNOW HOW MESSY THINGS ARE BEHIND THE SCENES.

NO MATTER WHAT . . .

MARCH

I DECIDED THAT I COULD PUT ON A SHOW, TOO.

HEY, I SAW YOUR NAME ON THE TRYOUT LIST. YOU FEEL GOOD ABOUT IT?
GOOD. GREAT. AMAZING.

WELL, YOU'VE ALREADY GOT MY VOTE.
THANKS, STEPHANIE!

RM 110

HEY, EVERYTHING OKAY?
WHAT? OH YEAH, NEVER BETTER!

HELLO, TEAM TOE!
COLOR WHEEL

I THINK OUR TOE FOREST NEEDS A GROVE OF PINKIES!

SOMEONE'S IN A HAPPY MOOD.
WHAT? WHO WOULDN'T BE INSPIRED BY OUR ARTISTIC ENDEAVOR?
NOW, THAT'S THE SPIRIT!

THAT AFTERNOON
ALL RIGHT, GIRLS! AS YOU'VE HEARD, WE'RE DOING THINGS A LITTLE DIFFERENTLY THIS YEAR.
YOU'LL TRY OUT IN FRONT OF THE EIGHTH GRADE STUDENTS, WHO WILL VOTE FOR THEIR TOP CHOICES. LATER THAT NIGHT, YOU'LL PERFORM FOR A PANEL OF JUDGES AT THE HIGH SCHOOL.
"THE JUDGES WILL SCORE YOU ON JUMPS . . ."
"TUMBLING . . ."
"YOUR CHEER TECHNIQUE . . ."

"AND YOUR OVERALL SPIRIT."
"SO LET'S SEE THOSE SMILES!"

UTILIT
GOOD JOB TODAY, CHRISTINA.
THANK YOU!

YOU KEEP THAT BIG SMILE, OKAY? THE JUDGES LOVE TO SEE HAPPY FACES UP THERE.
OH, I AM KEEPING THIS THING, 24/7!

MOM? DID DAD CALL?
NOT YET, SWEETIE.

YOU COULD CALL HIM AT SAM'S HOUSE.

I KNOW WHO TO CALL . . .
HELLO?
I NEED TO TALK. CAN YOU GET LEANNE ON THREE-WAY?
FLASH
REDIAL
TEEN
HELLO?
HEY, IT'S US.
HEY. I HAVE SOMETHING TO TELL YOU . . .

YOUR PARENTS?? WOW, I'M SO SORRY.
OH MY GOSH, SERIOUSLY?
YEAH. I KNOW.
SO DID THEY ACTUALLY SAY THE WORD DIVORCE?
THEY SAID THE MARRIAGE WAS "OVER." WHY?
WELL, SOMETIMES PEOPLE GET "SEPARATED."
RIGHT. THEY DON'T LIVE TOGETHER, BUT THEY AREN'T DIVORCED, EITHER.
AND DO THEY EVER GET BACK TOGETHER?
SOMETIMES.
I MEAN, IT HAPPENS ON TV.

HAD I ACTUALLY HEARD THE WORD DIVORCE? NO, I HADN'T.
"THAT'S IT! MOM AND DAD ARE 'SEPARATED.' IT SOUNDS KIND OF FANCY—AND DEFINITELY NOT FINAL."
YES, DAHLING, MY PARENTS ARE SEPARATED, BUT WE STILL HOLIDAY IN MONACO TOGETHER.

THE NEXT DAY AT SCHOOL
COLOR WHEEL
CHECK IT OUT! OUR TOE FOREST IS NEARLY FULL GROWN!
HELLO, WEE TOE-LINGS!
HEY, CHRISTINA, I HEARD YOU'RE TRYING OUT FOR CHEERLEADER. IS THAT TRUE?
OH YEAH, HA-HA. I GUESS I AM.
ARE YOU SERIOUS? DON'T YOU REMEMBER HOW DEVASTATED YOU WERE LAST TIME?
YEAH, WELL . . .
AND YOU WANT TO GO THROUGH ALL THAT AGAIN?
IT'S NOT A BIG DEAL.
. . . I DIDN'T EVEN WANT TO, BUT LEANNE NEEDED A PARTNER, SO . . .
WOW, THAT'S SO NICE OF YOU.
YOU KNOW WHO YOU ARE, CHRISTINA?

SAINT TOE-RESA.
HA-HA, YUP, THAT'S ME!
SO, CAN YOU ALL STILL COME OVER SATURDAY TO WATCH THE DARK CRYSTAL?
UGH, I CAN'T. WE'RE HAVING MY SISTER'S BOYFRIEND OVER FOR DINNER.
I THOUGHT THEY BROKE UP.
THEY'RE BACK TOGETHER. AGAIN.
LAST TIME SHE SWORE IT WAS OVER, BUT THEN TODD WROTE HER THIS MUSHY LOVE LETTER.
MY MOM JOKES THAT SHE ACTUALLY WROTE THE LETTER BECAUSE TODD IS THE ONLY ONE WHO LIKES HER COOKING.
HA, YOUR MOM IS SO FUNNY!
OF COURSE—A LETTER! THAT'S IT!

ONE OF MY FAVORITE OLD MOVIES WAS THE PARENT TRAP.
SHARON (PLAYED BY HAYLEY MILLS)
AND HER TWIN SISTER, SUSAN (THROUGH THE MAGIC OF SPECIAL EFFECTS, ALSO PLAYED BY HAYLEY MILLS!) . . .
REUNITED THEIR DIVORCED PARENTS BY PLAYING SOME AMAZING TWIN-TRICKS ON THEM.
THOSE TRICKS MADE ME WONDER WHY WE EVER SPLIT UP!
THANK GOODNESS THESE WACKY KIDS OF OURS GOT US BACK TOGETHER!

MY PARENTS JUST NEEDED A LITTLE HELP TO SEE THAT THEY ACTUALLY STILL BELONGED TOGETHER.
THE PLAN
WRITE A LOVE LETTER TO DAD, FROM "MOM"
WRITE A LOVE LETTER TO MOM FROM "DAD"
ARRANGE A MEETING IN A ROMANTIC SPOT.
LET THE REUNITING BEGIN.

UP

KNOCK! KNOCK!

HEY, LITTLE COUSIN.
NIKKI!

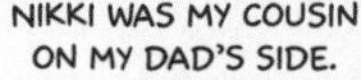
NIKKI WAS MY COUSIN ON MY DAD'S SIDE.

WHEN I WAS IN ELEMENTARY SCHOOL, HER PARENTS SENT HER FROM BANGKOK TO LIVE WITH US SO SHE COULD GET AN AMERICAN EDUCATION.
WE WERE REALLY CLOSE. LIKE SISTERS.
HOORAY, IT'S BARBIE TIME!
KEEP OUT!!
I TOLD YOU TO KNOCK.
BARBIES NEVER KNOCK. THEY JUST BARGE IN TO BE FABULOUS!
MO-OMM! NIKKI PUT A LOCK ON HER DOOR!
KEEP OUT!!

WHAT ARE YOU DOING HERE?
MY COLLEGE GAVE US A LONG WEEKEND, SO I THOUGHT I'D COME VISIT.
I TOLD YOUR DAD I'D BE HERE, BUT I GUESS HE FORGOT.
YEAH, I THINK HE'S STAYING AT A FRIEND'S HOUSE RIGHT NOW.
MOM AND DAD ARE, LIKE, "SEPARATED" OR SOMETHING.
OH MY GOSH, I'M SO SORRY.
NO, IT'S FINE! THEY'RE GETTING BACK TOGETHER.
REALLY?
YEAH, THANKS TO ME. YOU CAN HELP!
ARE YOU BETTER AT FORGERY OR LYING?
CHRISTINA . . .

YOU CAN FORGE THE LOVE LETTER, AND I'LL DO THE LYING.
CHRISTINA, I'M REALLY SORRY ABOUT YOUR PARENTS, BUT I'M NOT EXACTLY SURPRISED.

HUH?
WHEN I WAS LIVING WITH YOU, I HEARD THEM FIGHTING A LOT.

YOU DID? ABOUT WHAT?
ABOUT MONEY. THE RESTAURANT. YOU HEARD IT, TOO.

YOU CAN'T KEEP DOING THIS!
YOU MAKE EVERYTHING A BIG DEAL! IT'S FINE!

LET'S PLAY MUSIC REAL LOUD SO THE BARBIES CAN HAVE A DANCE PARTY!
YOU ALWAYS . . .
YOU NEVER . . .

THEY JUST ALWAYS SEEMED REALLY DIFFERENT TO ME.
OH.

I'M SORRY. I KNOW THIS HAS TO BE REALLY SAD FOR YOU.

WHAT? NO, I'M NOT SAD. IT'S JUST A SEPARATION. IT'S ONLY TEMPORARY.
UP

OKAY. WELL, DO YOU WANT TO EAT WITH ME?
OF COURSE!

THE PLAN

APRIL
LET'S GO . . . ROOS!
GREAT JOB! ALL RIGHT, SEE YOU TOMORROW, SAME TIME.
THE TRYOUT KEPT ME FROM THINKING ABOUT THE DIVORCE—I MEAN, THE **SEPARATION.**
THIS YEAR'S CHEER IS WAY HARDER.
AND WE HAVE LESS TIME TO LEARN IT.
I WISH PRACTICE WAS LONGER.
ONCE I GOT HOME, THOUGH, IT WAS UNAVOIDABLE.
I TRIED THAT . . . NO, IT DIDN'T HELP, EITHER . . .

YEAH, IT'S BEEN GOING ON FOR A LONG TIME . . .

I THINK YOU'RE EXACTLY RIGHT . . .

WE JUST DON'T BELONG TOGETHER.

AND WHAT ABOUT YOU? HOW ARE THINGS . . .

DON'T BELONG TOGETHER?

SURE, MOM AND DAD ARE REALLY DIFFERENT.

BUT DIFFERENT THINGS CAN MAKE A GREAT COMBINATION, RIGHT?

MOM AND DAD MADE ME WHO I AM. IF THEY DON'T BELONG TOGETHER . . .

WHAT DOES THAT SAY ABOUT ME ?

SWEETIE, IS THAT YOU?
UM, YEAH!

I WAS JUST TALKING TO JEANNIE DERMOND. SHE AND HER HUSBAND DIVORCED LAST SUMMER.
OKAY?

SHE'S INVITED US TO DINNER AT HER HOUSE.
UGH, MOM, THAT SOUNDS SUPER AWKWARD—

WAIT, DERMOND? YOU MEAN THE MOM OF **ANDY** DERMOND?
UM, YES, I THINK SO.

WE'RE GOING. IT'LL BE FUN, I PROMISE.
DOUBTFUL.

324
ONE WEEK BEFORE THE TRYOUT
SO THIS IS ANDY DERMOND'S HOUSE. WOW, IT'S REALLY NICE.

HELLO, Y'ALL! COME ON IN!
THANK YOU SO MUCH FOR HAVING US.
HI. YES, THANK YOU.

ANDY, YOU KNOW CHRISTINA, RIGHT? BE A GOOD HOST AND SHOW HER AROUND A LITTLE.
HEY.
HEY.

MY SISTER'S ROOM IS DOWN THE HALL. THIS IS MINE.

I CAN'T BELIEVE I'M IN ANDY'S ROOM. THERE'S HIS DESK.

THAT'S HIS BED. LEANNE AND MEGAN WOULD **FREAK OUT** RIGHT NOW.

GASP! HIS DEODORANT.

ANDY'S PARENTS JUST WENT THROUGH A DIVORCE.

WE ACTUALLY HAVE SOMETHING IN COMMON.
OUR SOULS ARE CONNECTED . . .
. . . AND SUDDENLY YOU FIND ME ATTRACTIVE.
LET US SHARE THE DEEPEST TURMOILS OF OUR HEARTS.
I CAN'T HEAR A WORD YOU'RE SAYING OVER ALL THIS WIND, BUT IT SEEMS VERY ROMANTIC!
SO. HUNGRY?
YUP.

THIS IS SO LOVELY, JEANNIE. WHAT A FEAST.
WELL, I REMEMBER HOW TOUGH IT WAS DURING MY DIVORCE.

TOO BAD **STACY** COULDN'T COME.
SHUT UP, LIZZY.

ANDY AND STACY SITTING IN A TREE, K-I-S-S . . .
SHUT **UP,** LIZARD TURD!

MANNERS!
NOW!

CHRISTINA, ARE YOU FRIENDS WITH STACY? SHE'S A CHEERLEADER.
WE HAVE NEVER SPOKEN IN OUR LIVES.
UM, YES, SORT OF.

CHRISTINA'S GOING TO TRY OUT FOR CHEERLEADER THIS YEAR.
OH REALLY? THAT'S FANTASTIC!
MM-HM.
I WOULD LIKE TO CRAWL INTO A HOLE AND DIE NOW.

I VOTED FOR YOU LAST YEAR.
YOU DID?

YEAH, I REMEMBER BECAUSE YOUR NAME WAS, LIKE, THREE TIMES LONGER THAN EVERYONE ELSE'S.

OH, WELL, TOO BAD MORE PEOPLE DIDN'T USE THAT METHOD.
ANDY, COULD YOU PLEASE PASS THE GREEN BEANS?

ZING!
OH . . .
WOW . . .

ONE DAY BEFORE THE TRYOUT
LET'S GO, ROOS! BEAT 'EM, BEAT 'EM!
ROOS!
WE CAN'T GET ANY BETTER THAN THAT!
WE ARE SO READY!
SO, EVERYONE FEELS GOOD ABOUT TOMORROW?
IF BY "GOOD," YOU MEAN TERRIFIED, THEN YES.
ALL RIGHT, WHO AM I GOING TO MARRY?
A-B-C-D . . .
K-L-M!

MAC POTTER! HA-HA!
EW, NO THANKS!
H! HANK MULLEN? NOT BAD.

A . . .
A FOR ANDY. A FOR ANDY.
WELL, WOULD YA LOOK AT THAT, IT CAME RIGHT OFF AT A!
ARE YOU BLEEDING?
NO.

I HAVE A GOOD FEELING ABOUT TOMORROW. WE KNOW THE CHEERS AND THE ROUTINE.
I FELT LIKE THAT LAST YEAR, TOO, AND WE ALL KNOW HOW THAT TURNED OUT.

NOT MAKING IT AGAIN IS TOO PAINFUL TO IMAGINE.
WANT TO KNOW SOMETHING WEIRD?

LAST YEAR I WAS SO STRESSED, BUT THIS YEAR, IT FEELS LIKE THE TRYOUT ISN'T REALLY HAPPENING.

IT'S MORE LIKE I'M WATCHING A MOVIE OF MYSELF GOING THROUGH THE MOTIONS.

ANYWAY, THE TRYOUT IS COMING FOR US TOMORROW MORNING . . .
WHETHER WE'RE READY . . .
. . . OR NOT!

BYE! SEE YOU TOMORROW!

HEY, MOM! TOMORROW I NEED TO—
OH GOSH, I HAD PLANNED TO CLEAN ALL THIS UP BEFORE YOU GOT HOME . . .

WHAT'S GOING ON?
WE CAN TALK ABOUT IT LATER . . .

NO. NOW.
YOUR DAD AND I ARE FINALIZING THE DIVORCE . . .

FINALIZING? BUT WHAT ABOUT—
AS PART OF THE AGREEMENT, HE'S TAKING THE HOUSE AND PAYING ME FOR MY HALF.

WAIT. SO WHAT DOES THIS MEAN?
I FOUND US A VERY NICE APARTMENT . . .
CHRISTINA'S BOOKS BOX 1
WE'RE MOVING?
WHY CAN'T WE STAY IN THE HOUSE AND DAD GET AN APARTMENT?
HONEY, I WON'T BE ABLE TO AFFORD THE MORTGAGE BY MYSELF. EVEN AFTER I FIND A JOB.

I KNOW YOU DON'T UNDERSTAND RIGHT NOW. BUT SOMEDAY, YOU WILL.

ALL EIGHTH GRADE STUDENTS PLEASE HEAD TO THE CAFETERIA FOR THE CHEERLEADER TRYOUTS.

OKAY, STACY AND DIANNE, YOU'RE FIRST. BRIN AND ISABELLA, GET READY!

I CAN'T BELIEVE WE'RE MOVING.
I CAN'T BELIEVE WE'RE ABOUT TO DO THIS AGAIN.

YEAH, THIS TIME WE'RE UP HIGH LOOKING DOWN ON THE AUDIENCE.

UGH, I STILL FEEL LIKE I'M ABOUT TO THROW UP!

WILL I BE ABLE TO BRING ALL MY STUFF?

WHEN WILL I SEE DAD?
WHAT IF I SPEW ALL OVER THE KIDS IN THE FRONT ROW?
ALLIE AND MEGAN, YOU'RE NEXT! CHRISTINA AND LEANNE, YOU'RE AFTER THEM!

GOOD LUCK, CHRISTINA!
HMM?

OH YEAH, GOOD LUCK! YOU'VE GOT THIS!
OH MY GOSH, OH MY GOSH.

GIVE A ROUND OF APPLAUSE FOR ALLIE AND MEGAN!

HOW ARE YOU SO CALM RIGHT NOW?
I DON'T KNOW. I'M JUST . . . NOT DWELLING ON IT, I GUESS.

HOW COULD YOU **NOT** DWELL ON OUR IMPENDING DOOM?
DON'T THINK OF IT LIKE THAT.

THINK OF IT LIKE YOU'RE ON A MOVIE SET.
OKAY GIRLS, YOU'RE UP!

LIGHTS.

CAMERA.
. . . LET'S HEAR IT FOR CHRISTINA AND LEANNE!

ACTION.

LET'S GO ROOS!
BEAT 'EM! BEAT 'EM!
WE CAN'T LOSE!
LET'S GO . . .
ROOS!

ALL RIGHT, I'LL PASS OUT THE BALLOTS TO VOTE FOR THE CHEER SQUAD NOW . . .

PSST! CHRISTINA, I VOTED FOR YOU!
REALLY? THANKS, CARLOS.

SO WHEN DO YOU FIND OUT IF YOU MADE IT?
LAST YEAR, THEY CALLED US ALL TO THE CONFERENCE ROOM.

THE PRINCIPAL TOLD US THE RESULTS, AND THE GIRLS WHO MADE IT RAN INTO THE HALL SHRIEKING.

WHILE THE REST OF US SAT THERE IN A CLOUD OF DESPAIR AND SHAME. AND WE HAD TO WALK PAST THE WINNERS.

WHAT KIND OF SICK HORROR MOVIE IS THAT?
APPARENTLY IT "BUILDS CHARACTER."

THAT NIGHT. THE JUDGES' TRYOUT.
CAFETERIA

THAT WAS BRIN AND ISABELLA. THEY WERE THE LAST ONES TO GO.

THEY WERE SO LOUD. WAS I LOUD WHEN WE WENT?
YOU WERE!
YES! WHAT ABOUT ME?
WILL THE APARTMENT BUILDING HAVE ANY OTHER KIDS?

NOW THE JUDGES TALLY THEIR SCORES AND ADD THEM TO THE STUDENTS' VOTES. UGH, THIS IS THE WORST PART.
I WONDER IF ANYONE VOTED FOR ME.
HOW LONG WILL IT TAKE TO GET TO SCHOOL?

LADIES, THE RESULTS SHOULD BE READY IN ABOUT TWENTY MINUTES.
OKAY, COACH MONROE!

HOW MANY MINUTES HAS IT BEEN?
FORTY-ONE SECONDS.
I AM **NOT** CUT OUT FOR THIS!

OKAY, IF I CAN POP TEN JOINTS, WE'RE GOING TO MAKE IT.

EIGHT . . . NINE . . .

TEN!
THERE! SEE?
NO, PLEASE JUST STOP.

I KNOW
I DIDN'T MAKE IT.
LEANNE . . .
DO YOU EVER FEEL LIKE YOU KNOW THE FUTURE, ONE SECOND BEFORE IT HAPPENS?

I DIDN'T TELL LEANNE, BUT I HAD THE SAME WEIRD FEELING.

BEFORE COACH MONROE POSTED THE PAPER . . .

BEFORE ANYONE READ A SINGLE NAME . . .

I KNEW THIS TIME WAS DIFFERENT.

WE MADE IT!

OH MY GOSH! WE DID IT!

LEANNE, TOO?
12

14

OH MY GOODNESS . . .

I MADE IT, TOO! I MADE IT, TOO!

I CAN'T BELIEVE IT! **WE MADE THE SQUAD!!**
CHRISTINA, IT'S JUST LIKE YOU SAID!
YEAH . . .

EVERYTHING IS PERFECT.

I ASKED FOR THIS UNIT BECAUSE WE'LL HAVE A NICE VIEW OF THE SUNSET.

WHOEVER LIVED HERE LAST TOOK REALLY GOOD CARE OF IT. EVERYTHING IS IN GREAT SHAPE.
IF YOU SAY SO.

HERE. YOU CAN TAKE THE BIGGER BEDROOM.

AND YOU CAN DECORATE IT HOWEVER YOU LIKE.

THE OTHER BEDROOM IS BY THE FRONT DOOR. THIS WAY, IF I HAVE TO LEAVE FOR WORK EARLY, I CAN SLIP OUT WITHOUT WAKING YOU UP.
OH, SO **THAT'S** WHY I'M GETTING THE BIGGER ROOM. FIGURES.

HEY, MEGAN, IT'S ME! YEAH, THIS IS OUR NEW NUMBER.

IT'S . . . JUST AN APARTMENT. MY MOM IS ACTING LIKE IT'S BUCKINGHAM PALACE.

WELL, TECHNICALLY SHE HAS CUSTODY OF ME. WHICH SOUNDS SUPER WEIRD.

BUT I'M SUPPOSED TO STAY WITH DAD ON THE WEEKENDS AT HOME . . . I MEAN—
THE PLAN

—AT OUR OLD HOUSE.
THE PLAN

I HAVEN'T SEEN HIM MUCH. HE'S BEEN STAYING WITH A FRIEND.
THE PLAN

BUT WHATEVER. WE'RE GOING TO BE SO BUSY WITH CHEERLEADING NOW.

I COULD CARE LESS.

MONDAY AFTER THE TRYOUT
LEANNE NEVER CALLED ME BACK. DID YOU TALK TO HER?
NO. I LEFT, LIKE, TWO HUNDRED MESSAGES OVER THE WEEKEND.
DO YOU THINK ANYONE ELSE AT SCHOOL KNOWS WE MADE THE SQUAD?
PROBABLY NOT. THEY HAVEN'T ANNOUNCED IT YET.
GOSH, REMEMBER COMING BACK AFTER THE LAST TIME?
A NIGHTMARE I CAN NEVER FORGET.

THERE THEY ARE!
HEY, CHRISTINA!
HI, MEGAN!
YOU THINK THEY KNOW?
LOOKS LIKE IT. WE HAVE TO FIND LEANNE.

THERE SHE IS. COME ON!
LEANNE!
HEY, WE WERE CALLING YOU ALL WEEKEND.
YEAH. SORRY.
I JUST DIDN'T FEEL LIKE TALKING.
WE UNDERSTAND.
I'M SO SORRY. I KNOW YOU DID AWESOME AT THE TRYOUT.
NO, I DIDN'T ACTUALLY. BUT IT'S FINE.
YOU'LL MAKE IT NEXT YEAR, I KNOW IT.
YEAH! YOU WILL!
⫶SIGH⫶ I JUST HOPE THAT—
SQUEEEEEEE!

MY SQUAD SISTERS!
MEGAN! CHRISTINA!
BRIN! WE'RE SO EXCITED!

DID YOU THREE HEAR?
WE'RE MEETING UP AT THE HIGH SCHOOL TOMORROW . . .
TO PICK OUT OUR UNIFORMS FOR NEXT YEAR!
WE GET TO PICK?

YEAH, THANKFULLY! LAST YEAR'S UNIFORMS WERE HIDEOUS!
AND YOUR MOMS SHOULD COME TO SIGN UP TO VOLUNTEER AND STUFF.
SEE YOU THERE!
OKAY!

WHERE DID LEANNE GO?
I GUESS SHE ALREADY WALKED TO CLASS.

CLASS! I GOTTA GO—SEE YOU LATER!
BYE!

PSST!
HEY!

GASP! IT'S ANDY!

CHRISTINA!
CONGRATULATIONS, CHEERLEADER!
THANKS.
I KNEW YOU WERE GOING TO MAKE IT. YOU WERE GREAT!
AREN'T YOU SO EXCITED?
I . . .
I MEAN, I GUESS. IT'S JUST SOMETHING FUN TO DO ON THE SIDE.
SO I WAS THINKING WE SHOULD HAVE ONE REALLY **BIG** TOE.
LIKE THE WISE OLD TOE OF THE FOREST?
YEAH, AND IT'S ALL GNARLED AND TWISTED.
OOH, WITH A BUNION!

THAT NIGHT
I DIDN'T REALLY KNOW BRIN THAT WELL BEFORE, BUT SHE'S SUPER SWEET.
THAT'S SO GREAT. I KNEW YOU'D—
AND ALLIE WILL PROBABLY BE OUR SQUAD CAPTAIN AND—OH!
TOMORROW NIGHT WE'RE MEETING OUR NEW COACH UP AT THE HIGH SCHOOL. MOMS ARE SUPPOSED TO COME, TOO.
OH, TOMORROW?
WE'LL PICK OUT OUR UNIFORMS. ISN'T THAT COOL?
SWEETIE, I CAN'T COME TOMORROW. I START MY NEW JOB AND I WON'T BE HOME IN TIME.
BUT THE MEETING'S NOT UNTIL FIVE P.M.
I HAVE TO DRIVE FROM FORT WORTH. I WON'T BE HOME UNTIL SEVEN.

WHY DID YOU GET A JOB ALL THE WAY IN FORT WORTH?
I COULDN'T FIND ANYTHING CLOSER THAT PAID ENOUGH.
I HAVE TO MAKE RENT AND PUT MONEY AWAY FOR SAVINGS. PLUS, I GET HEALTH INSURANCE.
BUT YOU'RE SUPPOSED TO VOLUNTEER FOR STUFF. ALL THE MOMS DO IT.
WELL, I'M NOT "ALL THE MOMS." AND I CAN'T DO THAT RIGHT NOW.
HOW AM I SUPPOSED TO GET TO THE MEETING, THEN?
MAYBE YOUR DAD CAN TAKE YOU.
YEAH, RIGHT. HE'S ALWAYS BUSY.
WELL, HE CAN FIND THE TIME.

SO, THIS IS GOING TO BE YOUR HIGH SCHOOL. WOW, IT'S SO BIG.
YEAH.

AND YOU'RE GOING TO BE A NINTH GRADE CHEERLEADER. THAT'S SO COOL, HONEY.
YEAH.

THE KANGAROOS, HUH? YOU KNOW WHAT MY SCHOOL MASCOT IN THAILAND WAS?
WHAT?

THE GRASS.
THE **GRASS?**

YEAH. OUR UNIFORMS HAD A PICTURE OF GRASS ON THEM.
SERIOUSLY? THE MIGHTY GRASS!

YOU KNOW WHO OUR RIVALS WERE?
WHO?

THE SOYBEANS.
NO WAY! THE FIGHTING SOYBEANS?

THEY WERE REALLY FIERCE.
AHA-HA! THAT'S HILARIOUS!

HONEY, I'M SORRY I HAVEN'T SEEN YOU MUCH, BUT I'VE BEEN REALLY BUSY.
UH-HUH.

I'M FIXING UP THE HOUSE. SO IT'S NICE WHEN YOU COME STAY WITH ME, OKAY?
'KAY.

HONEY, I—
THERE'S MEGAN.

GOTTA GO! BYE!

THERE WASN'T ANY REAL REASON DADS COULDN'T COME TO THE MEETINGS.

BUT LIKE MOST THINGS THAT HAPPENED AFTER SCHOOL...

IT WAS RUN BY MOMS.

EVERYONE, I'M COACH ELLEN, AND I'M THE HIGH SCHOOL CHEERLEADING SPONSOR.

EVEN THOUGH YOU WON'T START CHEERING UNTIL THE FALL, THIS IS YOUR OFFICIAL WELCOME TO THE GRANGEVIEW NINTH GRADE SQUAD!
OUR FIRST ORDER OF BUSINESS IS TO VOTE ON A SQUAD CAPTAIN.
I NOMINATE ALLIE. SHE'S ORGANIZED, SUPPORTIVE, AND HAS A GREAT ATTITUDE.
PLUS, IT'S A HARD JOB AND NO ONE ELSE WANTS IT.
GIRLS?
AYE!
THANK YOU! I'M DEEPLY HONORED!

ALL RIGHT, FIRST UP: UNIFORMS. THESE ARE THE CURRENT NINTH GRADE CHEERLEADING UNIFORMS.

ICK!
BARF-OLA.
UGH.
1992 CALLED AND IT WANTS ITS UNIFORM BACK.

AND THIS IS MY PROPOSAL FOR NEXT YEAR.

OOOOOOOH.

ALL WHO VOTE FOR THE NEW STYLE?
AYE!
SWEET POM-POMS, WE ARE GOING TO LOOK **GOOD!**

OKAY, MOMS, VOLUNTEER SIGN-UPS ARE IN MY OFFICE. ALLIE, TAKE THE SQUAD TO THE LOCKER ROOM AND GO THROUGH THE REST OF THE AGENDA.
YOU GOT IT, COACH!

—INTRODUCING—
THE SQUAD
Together for the first time!
COACH ELLEN WANTED US TO DO A NAME GAME, BUT I'M SKIPPING THAT.

OKAY, SO WHO CAN TUMBLE?
KELLY CAN DO AN AERIAL NOW!
AND WITH YOUR BACK HANDSPRINGS, WE'RE GONNA LOOK AMAZING!
lie, Megan, and Kelly
~THE~
YMNASTICS GIRLS
They'll make you flip!
And flip again!

BRIN IS
OUR LITTLE SWEETHEART
IT'S HARD TO BELIEVE SOMEONE IS **THIS** NICE!
MY MOM AND I MADE EVERYONE HAIR BOWS TO WEAR AT CAMP.

NOBODY TOUCHES MY HAIR.
YUP, GOT IT!
Laura stars as
THE GLAMOROUS TOUGH GIRL
You'll be kind of a little scared of her!

THE POPULARITY REPORTER
Meet Stacy and Dianne
TAKE THE QUIZ: WILL THEY LIKE YOU?
THE SCOOP: WILL WEDDING BELLS RING FOR STACY & ANDY?
HERE, LET ME HELP YOU.
THANKS!
OKAY, LISTEN UP. HERE'S A LIST OF ALL THE SUPPLIES WE EACH NEED TO BRING TO CAMP.
WATER BOTTLE . . . ICE PACK . . . PERSONAL FAN . . . HYDRATION TABLETS?
WE NEED **FOUR** BOTTLES OF SUNSCREEN?

I'VE NEVER BEEN TO A CAMP BEFORE. THIS WILL BE SO FUN!
BAHAHAHA!
YOU THINK CHEERLEADING CAMP IS **FUN?**
IT'S HOT. LIKE A THOUSAND DEGREES. NO SHADE.
YOU CHEER **ALL** DAY.
LAST YEAR, I HAD BLISTERS SO BAD I COULDN'T WALK FOR A WEEK.
IN OTHER WORDS . . .
THE SINGLE BEST EXPERIENCE OF MY LIFE.

EVERY SQUAD IS GIVEN A RATING AT THE END OF THE WEEK.
NO GRANGEVIEW SQUAD HAS EVER BEEN RATED BELOW FIVE STARS.
WE WILL NOT FAIL ON MY WATCH!
YES, ALLIE, CAPTAIN, MA'AM!
THAT MEANS WE CHEER HARD, AND WE LOOK GOOD DOING IT. YOU WILL WEAR YOUR KANGAROO SWAG AT ALL TIMES.
REMIND ME AGAIN WHY OUR HIGH SCHOOL HAS A KANGAROO FOR A MASCOT?
KANGAROOS CAN'T HOP BACKWARD. IT'S ONLY FORWARD, TO OUR GOAL!
AND IF THEY GET CORNERED, THEY FIGHT LIKE HECK.
YEAH, AND . . .

AND WHEN A BABY KANGAROO IS BORN, IT CRAWLS FROM THE BIRTH CANAL TO THE MOTHER'S POUCH.
ITS LIPS FUSE TO THE MOTHER, WHERE IT WILL REMAIN ATTACHED FOR FOUR MONTHS.
IN CONCLUSION, THEY'RE TENACIOUS!
AND WHAT?
YIKES, DO NOT LET THEM SEE HOW WEIRD YOU ARE!
. . . AND KANGAROOS ARE SO CUTE!

OH MY GOSH, CHRISTINA, LISTEN TO THIS!
IN CHOIR, I HEARD DANE SAY HE THINKS YOU'RE REALLY PRETTY!
TOBIN'S FRIEND?
YES, HE SAID "I WISH SHE WERE MY CHINA DOLL"!
UH . . .
JUST HAD TO TELL YOU! SEE YOU LATER!
WHAT A RACIST AND SEXIST AND TOTALLY GROSS THING TO SAY!
AM I SUPPOSED TO THINK THAT'S A COMPLIMENT??
OH GREAT, HERE COMES DANE NOW.
UGHHHHH.

HEY, CHRISTINA.
OH. HI.
SKATE

SO . . .

CAN I HAVE YOUR PHONE NUMBER?
NO.

WHAT DO YOU MEAN, NO?
I MEAN YOU CAN'T HAVE IT.

WAIT. **YOU** DON'T WANT **ME** TO . . .
YOU HEARD HER, DANE. LET'S GO.

FINE! I DIDN'T WANT TO CALL YOU, ANYWAY! YOU'RE NOT EVEN PRETTY!

WHAT A COMPLETE JERK!
SERIOUSLY. WAS I SUPPOSED TO BE GRATEFUL HE ASKED FOR MY NUMBER?
Science fair

YOU KNOW WHAT? PART OF ME IS **MAD** THAT SUDDENLY WE'RE BECOMING POPULAR.
RIGHT? LIKE, WHAT WAS WRONG WITH US BEFORE?

NOTHING! AND NOW THOSE BOYS EXPECT US TO JUST FORGET ALL THE MEAN THINGS THEY USED TO SAY.
I DIDN'T HEAR THE WORDS "I'M SORRY," DID YOU?

JUST BECAUSE THEY'RE POPULAR, TOO, ARE WE SUPPOSED TO BE FRIENDS WITH THEM?
NO **WAY.**

THEY DO NOT GET A PASS.

I'M RETURNING YOUR GRADED QUIZZES.

65

WOW, TOBIN. A SIXTY-FIVE, HUH?
UGH.

DIDN'T YOU FAIL THE LAST QUIZ, TOO?
SHUT UP.

THIS QUIZ WAS SUPER EASY. YOU MUST BE PRETTY STUPID.
I'M NOT.
ALL EYES UP HERE, PLEASE!

GETTING BACK AT TOBIN WAS SUPPOSED TO FEEL GREAT.

BUT NOTHING WAS FEELING AS GOOD AS IT WAS SUPPOSED TO.

OH, SORRY, CHRISTINA, I—
WATCH IT!
WHOA, RICE GIRL'S MAD!

LAST YEAR, I FELT LIKE THE CHEERLEADERS HAD EVERYTHING. THEY WERE POPULAR. THEY HAD A "GLOW."
THIS BOOK IS BORING. WHOEVER HEARD OF THIS AUTHOR, ANYWAY?
HOMEWORK ASSIGNMENT

YOU MEAN MARK TWAIN?
MORE LIKE MARK NO-BRAIN.
HAHA HA HAHA

NICE SKIRT, BONNIE. LOOKS LIKE YOU THINK YOU'RE A CHEERLEADER.
HAHA HA HAHA HA HAHA
BUT I WASN'T GLOWING.

COLOR WHEEL
I WAS BURNING UP INSIDE.

ARE YOU OKAY, CHRISTINA?
YEAH, YOUR FACE IS RED.

IT IS? UM YEAH, I'M FINE.

SO MY FELLOW TOE SHEPHERDS, HAVE YOU MADE YOUR ELECTIVE CHOICES FOR NEXT YEAR?
WE'RE ALL TAKING ART, RIGHT?

YES! I HEARD WE GET TO USE A REAL PHOTOGRAPHY LAB.
WE ARE GOING TO DO, LIKE, ACTUAL AVANT-GARDE THINGS.

WHAT'S WRONG, CHRISTINA?
UMMMM . . .

ART IS THE SAME PERIOD AS CHEERLEADING.

OH NO!
WHAT ARE YOU GOING TO DO?

WHAT DO YOU MEAN? I HAVE TO CHOOSE, DUH. SO I CAN'T DO ART.
BUT YOU LOVE ART.

I JUST MADE THE SQUAD, CARRIE. AM I SUPPOSED TO QUIT ALREADY?
YOU'RE SUPPOSED TO FOLLOW YOUR LIFE'S PASSIONS.
THAT'S EXACTLY WHAT I'M TRYING TO DO!
YOU'RE THE ONE WHO SAID THAT CHEERLEADING WASN'T A BIG DEAL.

YOU SAID YOU ONLY TRIED OUT TO HELP SOMEONE ELSE!
WELL, MAYBE I LIKE IT NOW!
CHRISTINA. THIS IS TRULY TRAGIC.
WHY? BECAUSE ART IS IMPORTANT, BUT CHEERLEADING IS DUMB? **HUH?**
THAT'S NOT WHAT HE MEANT.
BECAUSE YOU WON'T GET TO BE WITH US AND WE'LL MISS YOU. **DUH.**
TAKE A CHILL PILL, CHRISTINA.

UGH, I JUST WISH THIS DAY WAS OVER ALREADY.

HEY, CHRISTINA!
SIT WITH US!

UH, SORRY, BUT . . . I THINK I'M ALREADY SITTING OVER HERE.
OKAY!

UM, HI.

YOU HESITATED.
I DIDN'T! I JUST DIDN'T WANT TO BE RUDE.
DO YOU WANT TO SIT WITH THEM INSTEAD OF ME?
NO, BUT I AM ON A SQUAD WITH THEM NOW. AND THEY'RE NICE.

IF THEY'RE SO NICE, HOW COME THEY'VE NEVER WANTED TO BE YOUR FRIEND BEFORE?

HEY, WHAT'S GOING ON WITH THOSE TWO GIRLS?

I HEARD WHAT YOU SAID ABOUT ME!
YEAH, WELL, I HEARD WHAT YOU SAID ABOUT ME!

OH MY GOSH. ARE WE ABOUT TO SEE A . . .

FIGHT!!!!

Fight!
Fight!
Fight!
Fight!
KIDS! WE DO NOT STAND ON TABLES!
EVERYONE, SIT DOWN! STOP!
Fight!
Fight!
Fight!
Fight!
Fight!
Fight!
BUT WE COULDN'T STOP. AND THEN FOR SOME REASON . . .

FOOD FIGHT!
. . . WE ALL JUST . . . SNAPPED.

. . . THEN EVERYONE SORT OF WENT WILD. AND I MAY HAVE JOINED IN.
THE PRINCIPAL SAID YOU CHUCKED A PUDDING CUP TWENTY-FIVE YARDS. WITH SPIN.

IT'S NOT LIKE IT WAS MY IDEA. EVERYONE WAS DOING IT!
EVERYONE?
TEXAS

WELL, NOT LEANNE. SHE HID UNDER A TABLE AND RECITED THE PERIODIC TABLE.
IT DOESN'T MATTER IF EVERYONE DOES SOMETHING BAD, CHRISTINA. **YOU** HAVE TO DO THE RIGHT THING.

WELL, OUR ENTIRE GRADE HAS ASSIGNED SEATS AND SILENT LUNCH FOR TWO WEEKS. HAPPY?
CHRISTINA, I DON'T UNDERSTAND THIS ATTITUDE FROM YOU LATELY.

SWEETIE, I KNOW ALL OF THIS HAS BEEN REALLY HARD. I JUST . . . YOU DO KNOW THAT THE DIVORCE WASN'T YOUR FAULT, RIGHT?
TEXAS
ARE YOU KIDDING ME?
OF **COURSE** I KNOW IT'S NOT MY FAULT!
TEXAS
IT'S **YOUR** FAULT! AND DAD'S! BUT **I'M** THE ONE WHO HAS TO DEAL WITH IT!
I **SWEAR,** YOU JUST **DO NOT GET IT!**
SLAM

UGH, ASSIGNED SEATING FOR TWO WEEKS.
WORTH IT. THAT FOOD FIGHT WAS **LEGIT.**
YOU, SIT THERE. YOU, OVER THERE. I SEE WHAT YOU'RE DOING, STACY.

WHO? ME?
YOU THINK I DON'T KNOW THAT YOU AND ANDY SPACED YOURSELVES APART IN LINE SO YOU CAN SIT TOGETHER?

ROMEO, YOU CAN SIT OVER HERE. JULIET, YOU'RE OVER THERE.
DUDE!
OH MY GOSH!

EVERYONE WILL EAT IN COMPLETE SILENCE.

GIGGLE!

MAY
TIME SPUN ON TOWARD SUMMER.

WE PICKED ELECTIVES FOR HIGH SCHOOL.

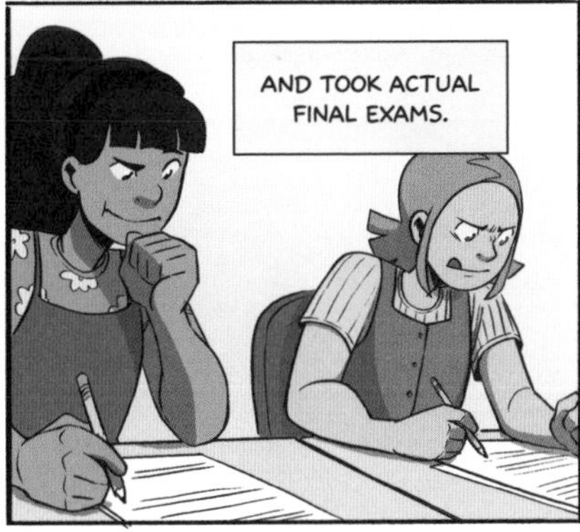
AND TOOK ACTUAL FINAL EXAMS.

WE DEALT WITH SHOCK WAVES.
Y'ALL, DID YOU **HEAR?**
WHAT?

STACY AND ANDY BROKE UP!
IS NOTHING IN THIS WORLD SACRED?
REALLY? GOSH, THAT IS **TERRIBLE.**

SOME THINGS FELT SO GREAT.

ROCK

SOME THINGS FELT REALLY BAD.

SWEETIE, YOUR DAD SAYS HE NEEDS TO POSTPONE AGAIN UNTIL NEXT WEEKEND. SORRY.

ALGEBRA TEST

ENGLISH DUE

STAY WITH DAD!

STAY WITH DAD!

STAY WITH DAD

AND OTHER THINGS FELT ALL MESSED UP.

BUT I DIDN'T KNOW WHAT TO DO ABOUT THEM.

I AVOIDED HANGING OUT WITH THE OTHER CHEERLEADERS.

LEANNE HAD A POINT—WHY HAD THEY NEVER WANTED TO BE FRIENDS WITH ME BEFORE?

WHAT IF THEY GOT TO KNOW THE REAL ME AND DIDN'T LIKE HER?

BYE, CHRISTINA, SEE YOU AT CHEERLEADING CAMP!
YOU BETTER START HYDRATING NOW.
YAY, WE'LL HAVE A WHOLE WEEK TOGETHER!
OH YEAH, HA-HA, A WHOLE WEEK, WOW CANNOT WAIT.

JUNE
MY COUSIN NIKKI CAME TO VISIT US ON HER WAY HOME TO THAILAND FOR THE SUMMER.
NIKKI!
YOUR FAVORITE COUSIN HAS ARRIVED.

DO YOU WANT NOODLES? CURRY?
ACTUALLY, I HAVE A DIFFERENT CRAVING IF THAT'S OK . . .

GROMS

TWO ORDERS OF FRIES AND TWO STRAWBERRY MILKSHAKES!
LARGE SIZES, PLEASE. WE'RE CELEBRATING AN EARLY BIRTHDAY.

Dip!
Dip!

SIGH

SO . . . DO YOU HAVE A BOYFRIEND?
NO! BUT THERE IS A BOY I HAVE A CRUSH ON.

OOOH, IS HE CUTE?
YES. AND HE'S ACTUALLY PRETTY NICE.

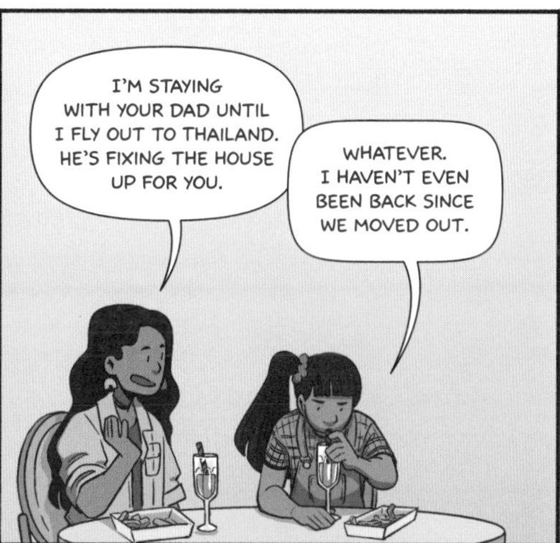
I'M STAYING WITH YOUR DAD UNTIL I FLY OUT TO THAILAND. HE'S FIXING THE HOUSE UP FOR YOU.
WHATEVER. I HAVEN'T EVEN BEEN BACK SINCE WE MOVED OUT.

ARE YOU DOING OK?
YUP, GREAT.

THIS YEAR IS SO WEIRD.
I ALWAYS HAD ALL THESE DIFFERENT PIECES OF ME THAT USED TO FIT TOGETHER, BUT NOW THEY'RE ALL SPLITTING APART.

I'M FINE WITH BEING A HALF KID. BUT NOW I DON'T EVEN KNOW WHICH HALF I'M SUPPOSED TO BE.
A HALF KID?

YOU KNOW. A LUUK KHRUENG. HALF A KID.
THAT'S NOT WHAT THAT WORD MEANS!

"IT DOESN'T MEAN YOU'RE HALF OF A PERSON."
"IT JUST MEANS YOU'RE HALF THAI."
"YOU DON'T HAVE TO CHOOSE. YOU'RE BOTH."
"AND YOU DON'T HAVE TO PICK ONE PART OF YOU. YOU'RE ALL OF THEM."
OH . . . OF COURSE.
WOULDN'T BE THE FIRST TIME I MISUNDERSTOOD A THAI WORD.
HEY, DON'T BE HARD ON YOURSELF.

WHEN YOUR DAD FIRST CAME TO AMERICA, HE WOULD PUT DIRTY CLOTHES IN THE DRYER WITHOUT WASHING THEM.
REALLY? WHY?
HE THOUGHT IT WAS "DRY CLEANING."
SERIOUSLY? HA!

ONE WEEK LATER

HAS DAD BEEN AVOIDING ME?
HONK! HONK!

GUESS HE CAN'T PUT ME OFF TODAY.

HEY, BIRTHDAY GIRL!
HI, DAD.

I'VE GOT LOTS OF PRESENTS FOR YOU.
MM, HMM.

HEY, IT'S OUR SONG—CCR! . . . "RAIN BEEN COMING DOWN . . ."
I KIND OF HAVE A HEADACHE. CAN WE TURN IT DOWN?

I GOT THE HOUSE ALL SET UP FOR YOU. YOU'LL LIKE IT.
IT'S SO WEIRD TO BE BACK HERE.

YOU PUT A POOL TABLE IN THE LIVING ROOM?
IT'S A SNOOKER TABLE! YOUR FRIENDS CAN COME OVER AND PLAY.

AND I GOT YOUR ROOM READY.
IT'S . . . CUTE.
BUT **SO** NOT MY STYLE.

SO, YOU WANT TO OPEN PRESENTS?
SURE.

WHOA, THESE ARE ALL FOR ME?
HEY, FOURTEEN IS A BIG YEAR.

YOU LIKE THEM?
ALL THE GIRLS AT SCHOOL WEAR THESE.

I THINK THIS IS A POPULAR PURSE RIGHT NOW.
WOW, YEAH, IT IS.
AND EXPENSIVE. HOW CAN HE AFFORD ALL THIS?

I CAN'T BELIEVE YOU'RE FOURTEEN ALREADY. WHEN I WAS YOUR AGE . . .
YOU WERE WORKING IN A NIGHTCLUB, BUSSING TABLES.

I WAS WORKING IN A NIGHTCLUB, BUSSING TABLES.
I'VE HEARD THIS STORY SO MANY—

IT WAS SO HARD. I NEARLY DROPPED OUT OF SCHOOL.

"I REMEMBER WHEN YOU WERE BORN, YOUR MOM AND I WERE LIVING IN THIS TINY RENTAL HOUSE."
"WE COULDN'T EVEN AFFORD FURNITURE."

"AND I THOUGHT, MY KID IS NOT GOING TO LIVE LIKE I DID. I'M GOING TO GIVE HER EVERYTHING I NEVER HAD, NO MATTER WHAT IT TAKES."

I TOOK SOME RISKS. BUT YOU HAVE TO TAKE RISKS TO MAKE IT IN AMERICA.

YOUR MOM DIDN'T UNDERSTAND, AND I PUSHED HER AWAY.

MAYBE SHE COULD, THOUGH. IF YOU TALK TO HER ABOUT IT . . .
HONEY—

YOU CAN MAKE HER UNDERSTAND! SHE MIGHT NEED SOME TIME, BUT . . .
HONEY—

CAN'T YOU JUST TRY? WE COULD STILL BE A—
HONEY, NO. WE CAN'T. WE TRIED TO MAKE IT WORK FOR A LONG TIME.

I MADE TOO MANY MISTAKES. AND WE GREW TOO FAR APART.

IT'S BETTER THIS WAY. FOR YOUR MOM AND FOR YOU.

I BOUGHT YOU SOME MOVIES. DO YOU WANT TO WATCH ONE?
I KIND OF JUST WANT TO GO HOME . . .
OH, ARE YOU SURE, HONEY?
YEAH, I JUST . . . HAVE A STOMACHACHE.
OKAY. I'LL GET A BAG FOR THIS STUFF.
HAPPY BIRTHDAY

THE NEXT DAY
. . . AND THERE'S A "SNOOKER TABLE" WHERE THE COUCH USED TO BE!
YOU'RE SURE YOU WANT TO GIVE ME THESE? THEY'RE SO EXPENSIVE.

YES, HE GAVE ME, LIKE, FOUR PAIRS. THE PURSE, TOO. I DON'T EVEN USE A PURSE!
WOW.

AND HE PUT ALL THIS BABY STUFF IN MY ROOM. WHAT WAS HE THINKING?

HE WAS PROBABLY TRYING HIS BEST.
HEY, WHOSE SIDE ARE YOU ON?

SOMETIMES, CHRISTINA, YOU'RE JUST SO SPOILED AND YOU DON'T EVEN KNOW IT.
HEY, THAT'S NOT—

I'M SORRY YOUR PARENTS GOT DIVORCED. IT SUCKS. BUT YOU ACT LIKE YOU'RE THE ONLY ONE WITH PROBLEMS.
YOU DON'T UNDERSTAND.

YOU THINK I DON'T GET IT? MY DAD LEFT WHEN I WAS A BABY. I NEVER EVEN KNEW HIM.

WHAT ARE YOU TALKING ABOUT? YOUR DAD LOVES YOU.
THAT'S MY **STEPDAD.** MY BIRTH DAD SPLIT BEFORE I COULD EVEN TALK.

OH . . . I . . . YOU NEVER SAID . . .
YOU NEVER ASKED. WHENEVER WE TALK, THE CONVERSATION IS ALL ABOUT YOU.

IT'S REALLY HARD SOMETIMES.
BUT MY MOM IS AMAZING. AND MY STEPDAD LOVES US BOTH SO MUCH.
WHEN I FOCUS ON THE BLESSINGS GOD GAVE ME, I FEEL SO LUCKY.
OH . . . I . . . ARE YOU STILL UPSET ABOUT IT?
OF COURSE I AM! BUT YOU'RE TOO BUSY BEING POPULAR TO CARE WHAT'S GOING ON WITH ME.
I KNEW THAT WHEN YOU AND MEGAN MADE CHEERLEADER EVERYTHING WOULD BE DIFFERENT.
YOU HAVE NO IDEA WHAT THIS FEELS LIKE.
MY TWO BEST FRIENDS. GONE, JUST LIKE THAT.
THAT'S NOT TRUE . . .
LEANNE? YOUR MOM IS HERE, SWEETIE!

I HAVE TO GO. THANKS FOR THE CLOTHES.
LEANNE . . .

CHRISTINA, DON'T FORGET ABOUT YOUR PRE-CAMP CHEER MEETING TONIGHT.

JULY
SCHOOL BUS
go girls! GO ROOS! Cheer camp here we come!!

YOU GOT YOUR PILLOW? AND YOUR BAG?
EXTRA PADS AND TAMPONS?
MO-OM! YES, I HAVE EVERYTHING.
SCHOOL BUS

SORRY, YOU'VE NEVER DONE A SLEEPAWAY CAMP BEFORE.
I'LL BE FINE! LOVE YOU!

CHRISTINA!
HEY! WAIT UP!

HOLD THE BUS! I SAID, HOLD THE BUS!
OUR DRIVER ISN'T EVEN HERE YET.
SCHOOL B
GO ROOS!
WE HAD TO BRING YOU THESE.
WE EACH GOT TO KEEP PART OF THE FOREST.
OUR TOE-LINGS?
WE THOUGHT THEY'D BE SMALL ENOUGH TO TAKE TO CAMP.
OH HA-HA, YUP, I CAN FIT THEM IN MY BAG.
SO DEEP THAT NO ONE SEES THEM!
CARRIE COULDN'T COME?
NO, BUT SHE WANTS YOU TO CALL HER WHEN YOU GET BACK.
LADIES! TIME TO HIT THE ROAD!
THANK YOU.
TOE'S COMPANY, THREE'S A CROWD!
JUST REMEMBER TO TOE THE LINE!

ALL RIGHT, GIRLS, TAKE YOUR SEATS.
LET'S GET THIS SHOW ON THE ROAD!
SCHOOL BUS
CHEER CAMP, HERE WE COME!

GUESS I'LL SIT HERE.

MEGAN IS ALREADY FRIENDS WITH ALLIE AND KELLY FROM GYMNASTICS.

WOW, SHE HAS NO PROBLEM BEING HERSELF AROUND THEM.

THERE'S PERFECT STACY WITH HER PERFECT BACKPACK. WHAT DO I EVEN SAY TO HER?
Time 4 Cheer!

OKAY, CHRISTINA, JUST START TALKING.
SO, ARE YOU—
OH, GUESS WHAT? WE ATE AT GOLDEN DRAGON LAST NIGHT!
OH REALLY?
YES, AND YOUR DAD WAS THERE. HE IS SO NICE . . .
UH-OH. I'VE HAD THIS CONVERSATION BEFORE . . .

"YOUR DAD IS SO NICE. AND HE'S SO LITTLE AND CUTE!"
HE'S A PERSON, NOT A HAMSTER!
"YOUR DAD IS SO NICE, AND I LOVE HIS GLASSES."
THAT'S SAM. NOT MY DAD. THEY DON'T LOOK ALIKE AT ALL!
"YOUR DAD IS SO NICE, BUT I CAIN'T UNDERSTAND A **WO-ORD** IN THAT ACCENT OF HIS!"
YOU SHOULD HEAR **YOUR** ACCENT!
YOUR DAD IS SO NICE. HE MAKES ME FEEL LIKE HE'S KNOWN ME MY WHOLE LIFE.
OH! YEAH, HE'S PRETTY GREAT LIKE THAT.
SO . . . I LIKE YOUR BACKPACK.
OH, THANKS. BUT LOOK.

MOM WON'T GET ME A NEW ONE UNTIL SCHOOL STARTS.
TIME 4 CHEER!
I LOVE ANDY!
SQUAD 4EVER
SORRY. ARE YOU UPSET ABOUT THE BREAKUP?
NO WAY! IT'S NOT LIKE I WAS GOING TO MARRY ANDY OR SOMETHING.
EVERYONE ELSE THOUGHT YOU WERE!
PEOPLE NEED TO GET A LIFE!
I'M MORE THAN JUST "ANDY'S GIRLFRIEND," BUT NO ONE SAW ME THAT WAY.
HERE . . .
IT HAS KIND OF A PUNK ROCK VIBE, DON'T YOU THINK?
HA-HA, I LOVE IT. THANK YOU!
TIME 4 CHEER!
I LOVE CANDY!

SCHOOL BUS
Go girls! GO ROOS!
FINALLY, WE'RE HERE!
WOW, A REAL COLLEGE CAMPUS!
WE'LL TAKE THIS ROOM!
I'LL HANG UP OUR DOOR POSTERS!
OOH, A MINI FRIDGE! PUT THE CHOCOLATE BARS IN THERE!
CHRISTINA!
COME CHECK OUT OUR ROOM!
OH, OKAY . . .
WOW, THAT'S A TON OF SNACKS.
THOSE ARE FOR LATE-NIGHT GAMES.
LAST YEAR, WE ALL STAYED UP TALKING AND PLAYING TRUTH OR DARE.

YEAH, IF YOU HAD ANY SECRETS BEFORE CAMP, THEY'RE ALL COMING OUT.
OH? REALLY?

YEAH, LIKE WHO YOU HAVE A CRUSH ON.
I CANNOT TELL HER I HAVE A CRUSH ON HER EX-BOYFRIEND!

ALLIE WILL MAKE US GO TO BED EARLY AT FIRST, BUT WE'LL BREAK HER IN.
TRUST ME, BY THE END OF THE WEEK, WE'LL KNOW EVERYTHING ABOUT EACH OTHER!

GIRLS! IT'S ALREADY FIVE THIRTY A.M. HUSTLE, OR YOU'LL MISS BREAKFAST!
IT'S STILL DARK OUT!

YAWN!

IS THIS EVEN FOOD?

OH WOW.
YUP, YOU'VE GOT SQUADS FROM ALL OVER TEXAS HERE. SOME EVEN COME FROM OKLAHOMA.
WHY DOES EVERYONE HAVE SUCH GIANT WATER JUGS?

OH. THAT'S WHY.

CHEERLEADERS, WELCOME TO YOUR NEW HOME!

FOR THE NEXT WEEK, WE DON'T LEAVE THIS FIELD UNLESS IT'S TO EAT LUNCH OR PEE.

UCTX

THAT'S COUNSELOR ADRIAN. HE'S ON THE COVER OF THIS MONTH'S **CHEER USA MAGAZINE!**

ARE YOU READY?

READY!

O-**KAY!**

YOU WILL DRILL CHEERS.
FIGHT THIS FIGHT!
YOU THINK THE CROWD CAN HEAR THAT? LOUDER!
FIGHT THIS FIGHT!
SLIGHTLY BETTER!
YOU WILL DRILL JUMPS.
THAT WAS THE LAZIEST PIKE I'VE SEEN SINCE 1987. GIVE ME FIVE MORE!
YES, COUNSELOR!
UCTY

AT THE END OF THE WEEK, ALL THE SQUADS WILL BE JUDGED ON ONE FINAL ROUTINE.
PART OF YOUR TOTAL SCORE WILL BE YOUR OVERALL TEAM SPIRIT. WE KEEP TABS ON THAT ALL WEEK.
UCTX

WE GOT SPIRIT, YES WE DO!
WE GOT SPIRIT, HOW 'BOUT **YOU?!**

WHAT IS THEIR PROBLEM?
THEY CANNOT BE SERIOUS.
DO THEY NOT KNOW HOW HOT IT IS OUT HERE?
SHUSH! DON'T LET ADRIAN HEAR YOU COMPLAINING!

ALLIE, I CAN'T JUMP ANY MORE. THIS HEAT IS BRUTAL.
EVEN MY ARMPITS ARE SUNBURNED.
REMEMBER WHEN THAT CLOUD BLOCKED THE SUN?
I LOVED THAT CLOUD.
ZIP IT! WE ARE GETTING THAT FIVE-STAR RATING IF WE HAVE TO DIE TRYING!
I WILL **NOT** BE THE FIRST GRANGEVIEW CAPTAIN TO COME HOME A **FAILURE!**
SHH! HERE COMES THE COUNSELOR!
YOU. I WANT TO SEE YOUR STRADDLE JUMP AGAIN.
UCTX
ME? OKAY.

I DON'T THINK I'LL BE ABLE TO WALK TOMORROW.

DAY ONE, DOWN. FOUR MORE TO GO.

WE'VE GOT SPIRIT, YES WE DO!

GET ME OUTTA HERE.

COME WITHIN PUNCHING DISTANCE, AND I'LL SHOW YOU SOME SPIRIT.

DAY TWO
THAT FIRST NIGHT, WE CRASHED HARD. THE NEXT MORNING . . .
HI! I'M HAILEY! I'M COACHING YOUR MORNING CLINIC.
OKAY, WE'RE GOING TO PRACTICE YOUR ENTRANCE: THE WAY YOU RUN IN BEFORE YOUR CHEER.
UCTX

TUMBLERS WILL DO THEIR BEST RUNS, AND YOU OTHER GIRLS WILL FOLLOW, SPIRITING.

OKAY, NON-TUMBLERS, SHOW ME YOUR RUN-IN.
LET'S GO, ROOS!
GO TEAM!
YAY!

WHOA, WHOA, NOPE.
GIRLS, WHERE ARE YOUR FACIALS?
FACIALS?
YEAH, BIG FACIAL EXPRESSIONS. LIKE THIS.
UCTX
OR THIS.
UCTX
OR THIS ONE IS MY FAVORITE.
I JUST WISH I COULD TUMBLE LIKE THE REST OF THE GIRLS.
ME TOO. ALL WE HAVE ARE OUR FACES AND GOOFY SPIRIT FINGERS.
OKAY, I'M GONNA NEED Y'ALL TO STOP RIGHT THERE.

Y'ALL ARE A SQUAD. IT'S NOT YOU VS. THE GIRLS WHO CAN TUMBLE.
WHEN YOU RUN OUT THERE, YOU HAVE TO GIVE THE VIBE THAT "OUR SQUAD IS AWESOME."
UCTX
"OUR TEAM IS AWESOME! OUR SCHOOL IS AWESOME! OUR WHOLE TOWN IS AWESOME!"
IF YOU DO YOUR JOB RIGHT, EVERYONE WHO WATCHES YOU WILL FEEL LIKE THEY'RE A PART OF SOMETHING BIGGER THAN JUST THEM.
BUT IT DOESN'T WORK UNLESS EVERYONE ON THE SQUAD IS ALL IN. GOT IT?
GOT IT!
YEAH!

DAY THREE
DOES THIS LOOK LIKE MEAT TO YOU?
DON'T LOOK. JUST CHEW.
SO . . . TIRED . . .

IGNITE . . .
ROOS!

CHRISTINA, COME ON, IT'S YOUR TURN!
TRUTH OR DARE?
DUPERSTAR
CHOCO

BRIN JUST GOT DARED TO SMELL MEGAN'S STRESS BALL.
I DESERVE A MEDAL FOR BRAVERY.
RAD!

OH, GOSH, I'M JUST SO . . . TIRED. I'M GOING TO GO TO BED EARLY, I THINK.

THIS IS EXACTLY WHERE I WANTED TO BE. SO WHY DO I FEEL SO . . . OFF? WHY CAN'T I JUST BE HAPPY LIKE EVERYONE ELSE?

DAY FOUR
THE STUNT YOU'LL BE LEARNING TODAY IS THE EXTENSION.
THE FLYER IS IN THE SPOTLIGHT, BUT THE MOST IMPORTANT PEOPLE ARE ON THE GROUND.
UCTX
THE BASES ARE THE POWERHOUSES. AND THEY HAVE TO BE IN PERFECT SYNC.
UCTX

THEN WE'VE GOT THE **BACK SPOT.** SHE CALLS THE STUNTS AND—MOST IMPORTANTLY—
ONE . . . TWO . . .
SHE PROTECTS THE FLYER'S HEAD.

STUNTING IS DANGEROUS. IF YOU MESS UP, PEOPLE CAN GET REALLY HURT.
YOU HAVE GOT TO STEP UP. COMMIT. AND FOLLOW THROUGH.
UCTX

AND **NO ONE** HITS THE GROUND.

MEGAN, WE WANT YOU AS A FLYER FOR SURE.
I'M READY!

CHRISTINA, MAYBE YOU SHOULD TRY BEING A FLYER, TOO.
ME? ARE YOU SURE?
JUST GIVE IT A TRY!
OKAY, YEAH. A FLYER. I CAN DO THIS!

STEP UP.
COMMIT.
FOLLOW THROUGH.
YES, CHRISTINA!
YEAH, YOU GOT THIS!
I'VE GOT THIS. I'VE GOT THIS.

I . . . DO NOT HAVE THIS.
WHUMP!!!...

CHRISTINA!
OH MY GOSH! ARE YOU OKAY?
BACK UP, Y'ALL! SHE NEEDS AIR!
I—I CAN'T BREATHE! I CAN'T BREATHE!
I THINK YOU JUST GOT THE WIND KNOCKED OUT OF YOU.
IT HURTS . . . IT HURTS . . .
IT HURTS SO BAD . . .

OH NO . . .

COACH ELLEN!

COME ON, CHRISTINA. LET'S GET YOU CHECKED OUT . . .

HERE'S SOME JUICE. DO YOU WANT TO CALL YOUR MOM?
THANKS, BUT I'M FINE. REALLY.
PEACE

THE OTHER GIRLS STILL HAVE TO FINISH THEIR ROTATIONS. YOU SHOULD GET SOME REST.
OKAY.
PEACE

IT'S BEEN GOING ON FOR A LONG TIME.
I MADE TOO MANY MISTAKES.

IT'S BETTER THIS WAY. FOR YOUR MOM AND FOR YOU.
I KNOW YOU DON'T UNDERSTAND RIGHT NOW. BUT SOMEDAY, YOU WILL.
YOU HAVE REACHED LEANNE. PLEASE LEAVE A MESSAGE!
1 2 3 4 5 6 7 8 * 0 #
CARRIE? HEY, IT'S ME.
OH HEY! HOW'S CAMP?

WELL, I FELL ON MY FACE FROM TEN FEET IN THE AIR, AND IT'S HOTTER THAN A POTTERY KILN OUT HERE.
HA! BUT YOU'RE HAVING A GREAT TIME, RIGHT?
I'M TRYING. I DO WANT TO BE HERE. MAYBE THIS SOUNDS WEIRD, BUT I REALLY LOVE CHEERLEADING.
IT'S NOT WEIRD. SORRY IF I MADE YOU FEEL THAT WAY.
ACE
I GET IT NOW—IT'S YOUR PASSION. YOU CAN HAVE LOTS OF PASSIONS.
YEAH. I THINK YOU'RE RIGHT. BUT . . .
I'M STILL NOT REALLY FEELING 100-PERCENT COMFORTABLE HERE, I GUESS.
YOU MEAN WITH THE OTHER GIRLS? JUST BE YOURSELF.

YEAH . . . SOMETIMES I FEEL LIKE THERE'S MULTIPLE VERSIONS OF ME.
WELL . . . DON'T FEEL LIKE YOU HAVE TO CHOOSE.
BE ALL THE VERSIONS. THEY'LL LOVE YOU.
I MEAN, I DO. AND I HAVE EXCELLENT TASTE, OBVIOUSLY.
THANKS. I MISS YOU!
WE'LL HANG OUT WHEN YOU GET BACK!
1 2 3
4 5 6
7 8 9
* 0 #

CAN I COME IN?
YOU'RE UP!
HEY, HOW ARE YOU FEELING?

FINE. BUT I MUST HAVE BEEN EXHAUSTED BECAUSE I SLEPT SO HARD.
WE FEEL AWFUL THAT WE DROPPED YOU!
IT'S OKAY. IT WAS MY FAULT, TOO. I'M NOT MEANT TO BE A FLYER.
NOW THAT YOU'RE HERE, WANT TO JOIN TRUTH OR DARE?
GIVE HER AN EASY ONE!
WHAT'S YOUR WORST FEAR?
BESIDES SMELLING MEGAN'S SQUISH BALL.

ACTUALLY . . . I'VE BEEN THINKING ABOUT MY WORST FEAR ALL DAY.

NO . . .
OH NO. YOU'RE AFRAID OF HEIGHTS AND WE MADE YOU DO THAT STUNT!

YOU'RE AFRAID OF BEING A FAILURE.
NO . . .

MY PARENTS JUST GOT DIVORCED.
I'VE BEEN HOPING THINGS WOULD GO BACK TO HOW THEY WERE BEFORE . . .

BUT I'M STARTING TO REALIZE THAT'S NEVER GOING TO HAPPEN.

WHEN MY PARENTS SPLIT, EVERYTHING GOT REALLY WEIRD AND MESSED UP.

REALLY?
YEAH. IT WAS BAD, BUT IT'S BETTER NOW.

MY PARENTS ARE DIVORCED, BUT THEY'RE STILL FRIENDS. I DON'T UNDERSTAND WHY THEY COULDN'T JUST STAY MARRIED.
IT CAN BE SO CONFUSING.

IS THIS THE REAL REASON YOU WERE CRYING SO HARD TODAY?
YEAH, I GUESS SO.

I'M SORRY YOU HAD TO DO FIFTY PUSH-UPS BECAUSE OF ME.
I WOULD HAVE KILLED YOU, BUT I THOUGHT YOU WERE ALREADY DYING.

CHRISTINA, THAT WAS AN EPIC TRUTH.
THAT WASN'T SO BAD. WHAT ELSE HAVE YOU GOT?
WHO'S YOUR CRUSH?

CRUSH? TRY **TRUE LOVE.**
OOOOOOOH!

LADIES, IT'S TIME THAT I TOLD YOU ABOUT GENE KELLY . . .
UH-OH, HERE WE GO.
IS HE THAT CUTE KID ON THE TENNIS TEAM?

DAY FIVE
OUR LAST DAY OF CAMP FLEW BY.
WE FINALLY HIT OUR STRIDE.
WE WENT ALL IN.
LET'S HEAR IT, ROOS!
GO, GRANGEVIEW!
SHOW US THAT SPIRIT!

WE FIGURED OUT WHERE WE EACH FIT ON OUR SQUAD.
FOR ME, THAT WAS ON THE GROUND.
READY?
READY.

ONE,
TWO . . .

AND GRANGEVIEW'S SCORE IN THE ALL-STAR SHOWCASE IS . . .
FIVE STARS!
WE GOT SPIRIT, YES WE DO!
WE GOT SPIRIT, HOW 'BOUT **YOU?**

I WANT TO HEAR ALL ABOUT CAMP DURING DINNER.
AH, IT ACTUALLY FEELS GOOD TO BE HOME.
CHEER CAMP

WHAT'S ALL THIS?
OH, JUST SOME THINGS I PICKED UP FROM THE HOUSE. I'M SORTING STUFF TO DONATE.
CHEER CAMP

YOU'RE DONATING THESE?
OH NO, THOSE ARE TO KEEP! YOUR GRANDMOTHER SOONTORNVAT GAVE THEM TO ME WHEN YOUR DAD AND I GOT MARRIED. AREN'T THEY BEAUTIFUL?

OH. I THOUGHT MAYBE YOU WOULDN'T WANT TO KEEP THE THAI STUFF.
I THOUGHT YOU'D BE HAPPY TO LEAVE ALL THAT BEHIND.
WHAT? NO! I'VE ALWAYS LOVED YOUR DAD'S FAMILY. I ALWAYS WILL.
CHEER

BUT DON'T YOU THINK THINGS WERE HARDER BECAUSE YOU HAD SUCH DIFFERENT BACKGROUNDS?
CHRISTINA, OUR PROBLEMS HAD NOTHING TO DO WITH YOUR DAD BEING THAI AND ME BEING WHITE.

PEOPLE FROM DIFFERENT CULTURES MARRY EACH OTHER ALL THE TIME AND IT WORKS OUT.
YEAH, THAT'S TRUE . . .

EVERY MARRIAGE IS ITS OWN STORY. AND YOUR DAD IS ALWAYS GOING TO BE A PART OF MY STORY, EVEN THOUGH WE'RE DIVORCED.
CAMP

WE'LL ALWAYS BE CONNECTED BECAUSE WE HAVE YOU. I WOULDN'T TRADE THAT FOR ANYTHING.

I'M GOING TO CALL LEANNE.
OH, I FORGOT TO TELL YOU—THERE'S A MESSAGE FOR YOU ON THE MACHINE.
CHEER CAMP
A MESSAGE? WHO WOULD IT BE?
UM, HEY, CHRISTINA.
THIS IS ANDY. ANDY DERMOND. I WAS WONDERING IF YOU WANT TO GO TO THE MALL SOMETIME? UH. CALL ME.
OH. MY. GOSH.

OH
MY
GOOOOSH!
DO YOU WANT ME TO TAKE YOU? I'M NOT WORKING SATURDAY.
YES, BUT— WAIT . . .
HMMM. ANDY NEVER CALLED ME BEFORE . . .
MAYBE HE ONLY ASKED ME BECAUSE I'M A CHEERLEADER NOW.
WHO CARES? I'M GOING TO THE MALL WITH ANDYYYYYY!

I CAN'T BELIEVE IT.
I AM AT THE MALL WITH
ANDY DERMOND.

HOW LONG CAN WE GAZE INTO EACH OTHER'S EYES WITHOUT SPEAKING?
I WISH THE WIND WOULD COME BACK AND DROWN OUT THE AWKWARD SILENCE!
WANNA GO LOOK AT SOME T-SHIRTS?
SURE.
RUNNING TURBO

DO YOU WANT ME TO BUY THAT FOR YOU?
NO. I WANT YOU TO BUY ME THAT HOBBIT HOME.
UH, IT'S OKAY. BUT THANKS, ANYWAY.
WANT TO GO UPSTAIRS?
SURE.

WHO CARES ABOUT TALKING?
WHO NEEDS WORDS?
WE'RE AT THE MA-ALL!

OH! I WAS JUST LOOKING FOR YOU. ARE YOU READY TO GO?
YUP!
YUP!
BIG SALE

FOUR SECONDS AFTER GETTING HOME
WHAT???
YOU KISSED ANDY DERMOND IN AN ELEVATOR! AT THE MALL! THAT'S LIKE SOMETHING FROM A MOVIE!
HA-HA, IT WASN'T QUITE LIKE THE MOVIES.
I KNEW YOU HAD A CRUSH ON HIM!
HOW'D YOU KNOW?
I'M YOUR BEST FRIEND. I KNOW THESE THINGS. SO ARE YOU GOING TO BE HIS GIRLFRIEND NOW?
HE ASKED IF I WANTED TO HANG OUT THIS WEEK. I SAID I HAD OTHER PLANS.

WHAT??
HE ACTUALLY SOUNDED RELIEVED. WE DON'T HAVE THAT MUCH IN COMMON.
NOW THAT I THINK ABOUT IT, I CAN'T IMAGINE YOU TOGETHER.
THIS YEAR I WANT TO HANG OUT WITH PEOPLE I CAN BE MYSELF AROUND.
ALL THE VERSIONS OF MYSELF AT ONCE.
PEOPLE WHO WILL ENCOURAGE YOU TO FART ON THE SQUISHY BALL OF LIFE.
HA-HA, EXACTLY! HEY . . . HAVE YOU TALKED TO LEANNE?
NO, BUT MAYBE SHE'S STILL AT CHURCH CAMP.

SUMMER
ROLLED ON.

UM, HI.
IS LEANNE
THERE?
JUST
A MINUTE . . .
LEANNE!

. . . UM, SORRY.
I THINK SHE WENT
TO HER COUSIN'S
HOUSE.
OH,
OKAY.

I COULD LIVE ON POPSICLES.
TOTALLY. THEY REMIND ME OF BEING A LITTLE KID.
THIS TIME NEXT MONTH WE'LL BE IN **HIGH SCHOOL.**
THAT SOUNDS SO WEIRD.
THESE ARE OUR LAST POPSICLES AS KIDS! THE LAST CHEESE PUFF DUST WE INHALE BEFORE WE GET ALL MATURE AND STUFF!
DO YOU EVER LOOK BACK ON A HAPPY MEMORY AND IT ACTUALLY MAKES YOU SAD BECAUSE IT'S OVER?
AND AT THE TIME, YOU DIDN'T EVEN REALIZE HOW HAPPY THE MOMENT WAS?

BUT IF YOU FOCUS TOO HARD ON HOLDING ONTO THE HAPPINESS, IT DISAPPEARS.
JUST BECAUSE A HAPPY MOMENT IS OVER, AT LEAST YOU HAD IT ONCE. THAT'S SOMETHING.
SOME ASTROPHYSICISTS SAY THAT ALL MOMENTS IN TIME EXIST SIMULTANEOUSLY.
WHICH MEANS THAT THE HAPPY MOMENT ISN'T ACTUALLY GONE.
IT JUST EXISTS ELSEWHERE IN THE SPACE-TIME CONTINUUM!
I LIKE THAT IDEA.
ARE YOU OKAY?
YEAH, I'M JUST . . . REALLY, REALLY HAPPY RIGHT NOW.

GREG . . .
WHAT ARE YOU
DOING?
CREATING A
MOMENT OF YOUTHFUL
JOY THAT WILL
LIVE FOREVER IN
SPACE-TIME!

AAAAAA!

OH. HEY.
CAN I COME IN?

I'M REALLY SORRY ABOUT EVERYTHING. I'VE BEEN A JERK.
I'M SORRY FOR CALLING YOU SPOILED. I KNOW YOUR PARENTS' DIVORCE MADE YOU REALLY SAD.

IT DID. IT **DOES.**

I THINK MAYBE I'LL **NEVER** NOT BE SAD ABOUT IT.

BUT I KNOW THEY BOTH LOVE ME.

AND THINGS ARE GETTING BETTER. I THINK HIGH SCHOOL IS ACTUALLY GOING TO BE COOL.
I CAN'T WAIT FOR THEATER!
OOH, WE CAN TRY OUT FOR THE MUSICAL TOGETHER!
YOU CAN'T SING.
YOU SING. I'LL DANCE IN THE ENSEMBLE.
YOU CAN'T DANCE.
OKAY **FINE.** BUT I **CAN** BE OVERLY DRAMATIC.
THERE YOU GO.
LET'S GO TO LUNCH TOGETHER THE FIRST DAY. YOU, ME, AND MEGAN, LIKE ALWAYS.
YOU DON'T WANT TO HAVE LUNCH WITH YOUR SQUAD?
YOU **ARE** MY SQUAD.

AUGUST
"YOU BETTER LEARN IT FAST . . . YOU BETTER LEARN IT YOUNG . . ."
"'CAUSE SOMEDAY . . ."
HONK!!
BE RIGHT DOWN, DAD!

Valley Garden Apartments

HEY, YOU DOING GOOD?
YEAH, GREAT!

AND HOW ABOUT YOUR MOM?
PRETTY GOOD. HER JOB'S REALLY BUSY, THOUGH. SHE WORKS A LOT.

YOUR MOM DOES SO MUCH FOR YOU.
YEAH. YEAH, SHE REALLY DOES.

HONEY, IT'S OKAY IF YOU DON'T WANT TO STAY WITH ME THIS WEEKEND. I KNOW IT'S NOT—
I BROUGHT MY STUFF! I CAN'T WAIT!

AND I'M GOING TO STAY THE WEEKEND AFTER NEXT, TOO. I DON'T WANT TO MISS ANY MORE, OKAY?
I'LL NEVER MISS ANOTHER ONE. I PROMISE.

SO, WHAT SHOULD WE DO TODAY? GO TO THE MALL?
OH, THE MALL, HA-HA. YEAH.
I DON'T REALLY FEEL LIKE IT . . .

WE SHOULD GO EAT SOMEWHERE.
CHINESE?
YES!

"HEY, TONIGHT . . . GONNA BE TONIGHT . . ."
OOH, CCR. TURN IT UP!

SEPTEMBER
BYE! SEE YOU TONIGHT!
SEE YOU THERE!
FOOTBALL GAME TONIGHT!

MOM? I'M HOME!

CHRISTINA,
THEY CALLED ME IN TO WORK THIS AFTERNOON. I'LL MAKE OVERTIME IF I STAY LATE. I'LL TRY TO MAKE THE GAME.
SORRY.

HI, MEGAN, IT'S ME. CAN YOU GIVE ME A RIDE TO THE GAME?
COOL, THANKS!

MMM.
THIS STUFF IS
GOOD!

Don't worry, Mom!
I got a ride!
You're the
best mom
in the world!
I love you!!

ROOS STADIUM
OUR FIRST GAME. CAN YOU BELIEVE THIS?
NO, I TOTALLY CAN'T.
OH GREAT, THERE'S TOBIN.
I THOUGHT HE WAS ON THE FOOTBALL TEAM.
HE'S FAILING A CLASS SO HE CAN'T PLAY.
REALLY?

EVEN THOUGH I COULD THINK OF SOME GOOD INSULTS FOR TOBIN, I KEPT THEM TO MYSELF.

I DIDN'T HAVE TO FORGIVE HIM OR BE HIS FRIEND. BUT I DIDN'T HAVE TO BE HIS VILLAIN, EITHER.

I WASN'T GOING TO LET ANYTHING RUIN THIS NIGHT.

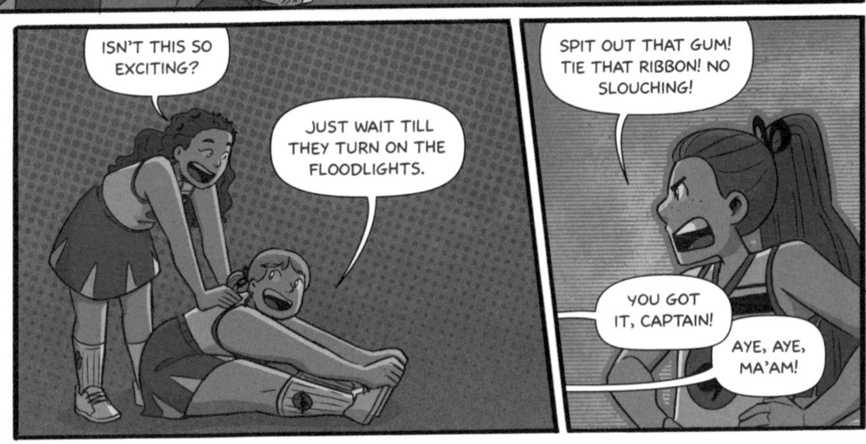

GET IN FORMATION! FROM NOW ON, WE'RE IN THE SPOTLIGHT!

ALL RIGHT, KANGAROO FANS, WHO'S READY TO MAKE SOME NOISE?
FLASH!
WHOAAAAA . . .
A YEAR AGO, I HAD SAT IN THOSE SAME STANDS AND WATCHED THE CHEERLEADERS PERFORM.

I HAD THOUGHT THEY WERE PERFECT.
READY?
O-KAY!
. . . BEAT 'EM! BEAT 'EM!
MAYBE THE PEOPLE WATCHING NOW WERE THINKING THE SAME THING ABOUT ME.
BUT NO ONE'S LIFE WAS PERFECT. THIS WASN'T THE MOVIES.
ROOS!

CHRISTINA!
MOM! HI!
I DIDN'T NEED LIFE TO BE PERFECT.

GO, CHRISTINA!
CHRISTINA! OVER HERE!
WOO-HOO!
I JUST NEEDED MY SQUAD.

AUTHOR'S NOTE

When I was younger, I always felt a little out of place wherever I was. In the small Texas town where I grew up, I was one of the only Asian American kids in my school. And when my family and I hung out with our Thai American community, I was one of the only biracial children there. But I always felt just right when I was with my parents; everything made sense when our family was together. And then suddenly, my mom and dad were splitting up, and that safe, comfortable world didn't exist anymore. Divorce was the hardest thing I ever went through. It made trying out for cheerleader feel like a cake walk.

Today, I understand that my parents were unhappy in their marriage for a lot longer than I realized. As an adult, I can see that it was the right decision for them to divorce. But at the time, I was so confused. Why couldn't they just work things out and stay together? Why couldn't everything keep *being the same*?

Middle school is already such a confusing and emotional time, and the divorce amplified every emotion. I made things even harder by trying to cover up my feelings. If you had gone to school with me in eighth grade, you might have thought I had it all together and lived a picture-perfect life. The funny thing is, I looked at all the *other kids* in my school and thought *they* had perfect lives, when really, so many of us were walking around, carrying all these burdens and not letting them show—until they exploded out of us, like on that day we had the epic lunchroom food fight (for the record, I do not condone chucking a pudding cup across a room for any reason).

I think that my eighth-grade self would have benefitted from talking to a therapist about the divorce, but thirty years ago in my small town, children's therapists were hard to find. Things are better today. If you're going through something hard and the emotions feel overwhelming, a therapist may be able to help you work through them. You can also talk to your own "squad." Lean on the trusted adults in your life: a family member or a school counselor, your teacher or librarian. You can talk to your friends and encourage them to talk to you, too.

It's normal to think you are alone in what you're feeling, but I promise you are not. And if you ever have thoughts about hurting yourself or someone else, definitely talk to an adult right away.

The events in this book really happened, though I'm sure I have made mistakes in reconstructing my memories. One of the hardest parts about writing this story was leaving people out. There were a lot of friends and a lot of great moments I didn't have room to include. I also had to shift around the timelines of some events so that they could fit in these pages. When I finally started telling friends at school about my struggles with my parents' divorce, it didn't happen all at once as I've depicted here. It took me time to feel comfortable sharing my feelings with people I trusted.

As for the rest of the story? Yes, I really did have my first smooch in an elevator at the mall. And I really did fall on my face at cheerleading camp and have a complete meltdown afterward. And yes, I actually had a long-standing crush on the actor Gene Kelly.

I still have fun watching old movies from Hollywood's "golden age," but now I see them with fresh eyes. I notice the offensive ways they portrayed women and people of color (if people of color even got to be onscreen). Until very recently, movies and television depicted Asians and Asian Americans almost entirely in stereotypes. I am sure that the boys who called me a "China doll" had been fed those same stereotypical versions of Asian women, which continue to affect how we are treated today.

Even when the old movies weren't being offensive, they still weren't very realistic. Every actor played a "perfect" part, and every story got wrapped up in a perfect, tidy bow at the end. Life is not like a movie. It's not like a book, either, even when it's a memoir.

This book ends, but my life has kept going on and on with lots of ups and downs. Even today, I continue to work through what my parents' divorce meant for me. I think a small part of me will always be sad about it. But I have also realized that having a squad that shifts and changes is a part of life, and it can even be wonderful.

It took time to get there, but today, both my parents live happy lives apart from each other. I am very lucky that they have both loved and supported me throughout my whole life. They are remarried, and now I have two fantastic stepparents and a big extended family. My husband and I have two daughters who are going through their own middle school years. We have a wonderful squad. But even so, our story is not over. It keeps going on with its own ups and downs.

If you are down, I promise things will go up again. And if you are up, look around to see if there is anyone on your own squad who could use a little boost.

As always, I'm cheering for you.

Christina

PHOTOS FROM CHRISTINA'S CHILDHOOD

My official cheerleading photo

My mom, dad, and me when I was seven months old

My mom, dad, and me with the agent who sold my parents their first home

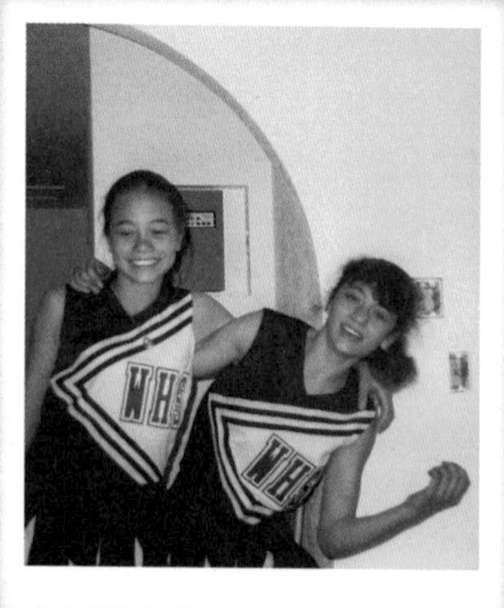

Megan and me when we first got our uniforms

Our 9th grade cheerleading squad

Our cheerleading squad at camp. I'm in the back row, second from right. Megan stands in the back on the far left.

Leanne and me at a pool party
the summer after eighth grade

My cousin Nikki and me in 1990
(when we had matching perms)

Christina
Writing

Sam Houston
Jan. 6, 1989

A day with Gene Kelley

One day I was going to the cafe, I was spending a day with the famous tapdancer; Gene Kelley. When I got to the cafe I was shaking all over. "Table for one maddamozeller," questioned the waiter. "No," "I am meeting someone." I replied. I walked to the dinning room, and sitting infront of me was Gene Kelley!!! I walked down to meet him, "Well," said mr. Kelley, "I thought you'd be taller." he said "Runs in the family". I replied calmly. First we ate, then we talked. At 4:00 I'd be going home so I wanted to ask one more question - How does he tapdance so well? So I asked; "Sir," "How do you dance so well?" "I never wash my feet." he said. After we goodbye I left and went

For one of my third-grade assignments, I wrote about an imaginary meeting with Gene Kelly in a Paris cafe.

AUTHOR'S ACKNOWLEDGMENTS

Once again, Joanna Cacao, thank you for bringing this story to such vivid life with your incredible art. You render every hilarious high and every emotional low moment so perfectly, and I'm so grateful to get to work with you.

To our letterer, Jesse Post, and colorist, Wes Dzioba, thank you for your brilliance. This is just the dream graphic novel team in every way.

So many thanks to our wonderful editor, Tracy Mack, who never loses sight of the heart of the story and helps make every book ring true. I'm so lucky I get to work with you! Thank you to our incredible squad at Scholastic and Graphix: Leslie Owusu, Phil Falco, Larsson McSwain, David Saylor, Brooke Shearouse, Cassandra Pelham Fulton, Elizabeth Krych, Elizabeth Palumbo, Emily Heddleson, Lizette Serrano, Erin Berger, Seale Ballenger, Dan Moser, Michael Strouse, Matt Poulter, and Meaghan Finnerty. Give me a megaphone, and I'll shout your praises all day!

Thank you to the wonderful Stephanie Fretwell-Hill, for making it possible for me to tell this story and so many more. And thank you to Jodi Reamer for being this book's champion and cheerleader.

I would not be who I am today without the good people I grew up with. Erica, Shauna, Carolyn, Leah, and Sara, no one in the world knows me like you do. I wouldn't trade our years together for anything in the universe. The Spirit Award goes to my kidlit squad. So grateful that I can lean on you for laughs and solidarity, Minh, Ellen, and Hena. And to my Stats and the Rosebuds friends, I love you all and we *are* doing that human pyramid one day!

Enormous gratitude to my whole family. Elowyn and Aven, thank you for making me a mom and a writer. You are in every story I write. Tom, I am grateful every day that I have your love. Bob and Liz, I am so glad that my squad grew to include you! And to Mom and Dad, I don't think I can ever thank you enough for all you have done for me. Your love and support mean everything to me, and I love you.

ILLUSTRATOR'S ACKNOWLEDGMENTS

MAJOR thanks to Christina Soontornvat for continuing to trust me with her story. It's been such a pleasure to draw these characters in relatable scenarios and to bring their emotions and feelings to life. Thank you to letterer, Jesse Post, and colorist, Wes Dzioba, who helped bring the book to its finish line, and for doing such amazing work, the best I could ever dream of.

Thank you to the Scholastic squad, specifically Phil Falco, Tracy Mack, Leslie Owusu, and Larsson McSwain, for making this book the best it could be. And to all those behind the scenes: Elizabeth Palumbo, David Saylor, Cassandra Pelham Fulton, Brooke Shearouse, Elizabeth Krych, Emily Heddleson, Lizette Serrano, Erin Berger, Seale Ballenger, Dan Moser, Michael Strouse, Matt Poulter, and Meaghan Finnerty, thank you for all your hard work!

Thank you to my agent, Tara Gilbert, who is the greatest cheerleader in my life. Thank you to my family and friends who love and support me. And last but not least, thank you to the love of my life, Warren Lacaba, who did all the chores during crunch time so that I could focus on drawing.

Photo by Sam Bond Photography

CHRISTINA SOONTORNVAT is a three-time Newbery Honoree, a Sibert Honoree, and a Kirkus Prize winner. She grew up reading books behind the counter of her parents' Thai/Chinese restaurant in a small Texas town. On why she writes about her middle school self: "My very happiest and most painful memories all come from those years. The funny thing is that I thought I had the world's most *boring* life. Only now do I realize that every day was full of stories." Christina's squad includes her husband, two daughters, a rascally cat, and an even more rascally dog.

JOANNA CACAO is a Canadian Filipino author-illustrator who loves working on magical and fantastical stories. She is the creator of the fantasy graphic novel *The Secret of the Ravens*, as well as many middle grade and YA webcomics. Though Joanna was never a cheerleader, her eldest sister was, so the world is familiar. She attended schools with predominantly white populations, where she experienced very similar situations to Christina. Joanna's squad includes her fiance and their two fluffy pups, Arya and Danny.

Photo by Warren Lacaba

In memory of my uncle, Donis Westmoreland,
beloved by his family and community.

CS

For all the kids; keep being you.

JC

Library of Congress Control Number: 2023045444

ISBN 978-1-338-74132-2 (hardcover)
ISBN 978-1-338-74131-5 (paperback)

10 9 8 7 6 5 4 3 2 1 24 25 26 27 28

Printed in China 62
First edition, November 2024
Edited by Tracy Mack
Lettering by Jesse Post
Coloring by Wes Dzioba
Book Design by Larsson McSwain
Creative Director: Phil Falco
Publisher: David Saylor